The Housefly Effect

**How Nudge Psychology
Steers our Behaviour
(without us even knowing!)**

The Housefly Effect

**Eva van den Broek
& Tim den Heijer**

Translated by Anna Asbury & Laura Vroomen

First published in The Netherlands in 2021 by Het Spectrum bv,
an imprint of Unieboek, Amsterdam

First published in the UK in 2024 by Bedford Square Publishers Ltd,
London, UK

bedfordsquarepublishers.co.uk
@bedsqpublishers

© Eva van den Broek & Tim den Heijer, 2024

English language translation copyright © Anna Asbury and Laura Vroomen, 2024

The right of Eva van den Broek & Tim den Heijer to be identified as the authors of this work has been asserted in accordance with the Copyright, Designs and Patents Act 1988. All rights reserved. No part of this book may be reproduced, stored in or introduced into a retrieval system, or transmitted, in any form or by any means (electronic, mechanical, photocopying, recording or otherwise) without the written permission of the publishers.

Any person who does any unauthorised act in relation to this publication may be liable to criminal prosecution and civil claims for damages.
A CIP catalogue record for this book is available from the British Library.

The manufacturer's authorised representative in the EU for product safety is Easy Access System Europe, Mustamäe tee 50, 10621 Tallinn, Estonia
gpsr.requests@easproject.com

ISBN
978-1-83501-144-7 (Paperback)
978-1-83501-142-3 (Hardback)
978-1-83501-208-6 (Trade paperback)
978-1-83501-143-0 (eBook)

2 4 6 8 10 9 7 5 3 1

Typeset in Utopia by Palimpsest Book Production Ltd, Falkirk, Stirlingshire

Printed in Great Britain by CPI Group (UK) Ltd, Croydon CR0 4YY

Contents

INTRODUCTION: 1
The world's most famous fly

CHAPTER 1:   11
Our deceptive brain

CHAPTER 2:   35
The power of convenience

CHAPTER 3:   67
Pain and how to turn it into gain

CHAPTER 4:   87
Conforming – are you doing it too?

CHAPTER 5:   117
Time has wings

CHAPTER 6:   145
The force of attraction

CHAPTER 7: 185
Money and motivation,
punishment and penalties

Epilogue 205

Acknowledgements 211

About the authors 213

Glossary 214

Bibliography 222

Introduction: The world's most famous fly

The natural habitat of the world's most famous fly is Amsterdam Schiphol Airport. Male travellers may have seen it many times, whereas women may pass through blissfully unaware, as you won't find this fly buzzing around in the air, or mounted in a glass cabinet, but in the urinals. That's right, we're talking about one of those painted flies in the gents'. The little fly first appeared in the airport in the early 1990s, but the idea wasn't altogether new. In Stratford-upon-Avon you can admire urinals with bees painted onto them dating back to around 1880, exemplifying typical British humour, as the Latin for bee, *apis*, sounds rather like what you'd use the urinal for. In the 1950s the Dutch army similarly had urinals with a little target inside. The fly in the airport toilet serves the same purpose: it gets men to aim more accurately, which doesn't happen otherwise – especially with jetlag, in transit – requiring cleaners to come and go with mops and buckets, in turn raising costs for the airport and inconveniencing flustered travellers faced with a closed toilet. The little fly gives men something to aim at, and it works, reducing 'splashback', the technical term for what ends up on the bathroom floor, by 50 percent. The cleaning costs also dropped substantially.[1]* That's why this insect has been emulated

---

* In an interview one spokesperson estimated the saving at 8 percent of the total

worldwide, and in other forms too, from a little goal net to competitive digital games. In Iceland after the banking crisis you could even aim at the faces of bankers.

Nevertheless the fly is far more famous in a field completely separate from hygiene: that of the behavioural sciences. Such a simple fake fly defies every classic 'rule' of behavioural change. Since the ancient Greeks and Romans, those rules have read roughly as follows: if you want to change someone's behaviour, you offer well chosen, clearly worded and carefully structured information and arguments (logos); you package these in an emotionally convincing manner (pathos); and you explain what makes you a credible messenger (ethos). It sounds as if it might work, and sometimes it does, but often it doesn't. No matter how clearly you explain to people that smoking is unhealthy – no matter which celebrity, scientist or influencer tells the story, or how moving, urgent or funny the commercials may be – a great many smokers continue to smoke. Behavioural change is a massive challenge.

A secret steer

The fact that it's so difficult to adjust behaviour is a serious problem, because whether you stop to think about it or not, we all try to do it, generally without dishonest or malicious intent. The truth is, humans are herd animals through and through; we need each other to achieve anything. So we have to ensure that colleagues work well together, citizens stick to the rules and customers buy things. It's the dentist's job to make sure you floss, the fundraiser's to persuade you to support the good cause and the DJ's to get you

---

toilet cleaning costs. That total of course includes far more than the urinals: women's toilets, cubicles in the men's, etc. He declined to attribute a monetary value to the saving, but we've read figures of as much as 35,000 euros per year. Meanwhile – in case you were wondering – Schiphol Airport is working on other innovations, such as sensors to indicate when a toilet needs cleaning.

Introduction: The world's most famous fly

to throw your arms in the air on the dance floor. People have to spur each other into action. But how do you achieve that when arguments and information aren't working? Threats? Coercion? Such methods might be appropriate for the army and the police, but not so much for selling shampoo. Bribery, then, with gifts, discounts and bonuses? They sometimes work, but often they're counterproductive (a matter we'll return to in detail later), and then you're left picking up the – devalued – pieces.

So what's the solution? That's where behavioural scientists, like Eva, come into play, along with advertising creatives, like Tim. They see that, oddly enough, that silly little fly really is effective. No stick or carrot, and yet that coveted behavioural change materialises.* So how does it work? The fly in the pot is often cited as the textbook example of a nudge, made famous by Nobel Prize winner Richard Thaler. Loosely defined, it's a small change in the environment that makes the desired behaviour easier, more fun or the obvious choice. Aiming at the fly is not the result of a conscious thought process, but seems to follow 'naturally'.

It's really not so exceptional when you think about it. In fact, your behaviour is being secretly nudged everywhere all the time, often by things so ordinary you never even stop to think about them. In the shops you take the familiar brand within easy reach. You book the holiday destination with guaranteed warm weather and head for the restaurant where you see the most people sitting. In the supermarket you start out sticking to the plan with lettuce and tomato, but you sneak a last-minute chocolate bar into the trolley when you reach the checkout. You're willing to pay a bit extra for a T-shirt from your favourite brand. And on your way home you'll take a detour to come in at just over 10,000 steps. It all seems so normal, but in all those cases your behaviour is influenced by something you barely notice. When something

---

* No logos, ethos or pathos, just apis.

apparently small has a big effect on people's actions, we call it the **housefly effect**, inspired by that fly in the toilet, but also by the **butterfly effect**. You know, that butterfly flapping its wings in Florence and setting off a chain reaction that culminates in a tornado in Texas. It's reassuring to know that the housefly effect is far more predictable, which means you can learn to recognise it, sometimes avoid it and often deploy it in a targeted fashion.

What we mean by houseflies and housefly effects

It's worth noting here that a housefly isn't some complicated mechanism in your brain (although it does start there). It's simply something researchers see happen in the world. For instance, when the arrows on traffic signs point upwards, there are fewer traffic jams than when they point downwards. When you give that fish a different name, people suddenly eat far more of it! What all these cases have in common is that something small has a huge effect on behaviour. In this book we call that small 'something' the housefly. So the fact that students borrow far less money when you remove a little asterisk on a website is a housefly effect. We call the asterisk itself the fly. Often such effects have been extensively researched by behavioural scientists and have received their own labels. In such cases we mention the names, as they help spread the story. Instead of saying we should 'do something different from the competition to stand out', advertising expert Tim says we should 'use the Von Restorff effect'. Sounds good, right? And behavioural scientist Eva would probably struggle to convince policy makers when saying that 'people like doing nothing', but gets a more positive reception for 'inertia causes people to be drawn to the default option'. In short, if you find the terms useful or fun, then hang on to them. We've indicated them with a little **fly**, so you can locate them easily in the text. They can also be found in the glossary at the back.

Introduction: The world's most famous fly

Houseflies come in all shapes and sizes, and we'll introduce you to a great many of them in this book, from the sneaky houseflies used by the supermarkets to fill your basket, to the kind of houseflies that get you to drive more safely or help you live a healthier life. We show you which houseflies you're better off avoiding due to their association with politicians, pickup artists and casinos, and which flies you can use to get your friends to come to your favourite restaurant, or your child to clear their plate. All the while we'll be using these effects on you as well, as you read this book. We'll (mostly) give you due notice. What do you think of the **effect effect**, for example? This housefly effect amounts to people finding something more interesting if you call it an effect. That's right: the title of this book isn't a complete coincidence.

But first this

In this book we'll be sharing a whole load of scientific insights with you, and we'll do our best to share responsibly and in manageable chunks. We want to inspire you and set you alight with our fascination for human behaviour and the science behind it. In order to do that, we sometimes have to simplify things. Not too much, but enough to make the book useful and readable. We do so consciously, although we occasionally have qualms when there's so much more to say! Still, we always do so with the best of intentions.

So if you know your way around the subject matter and feel we've oversimplified things, you're probably right. Don't take what we say about the brain, for instance, as a starting point for brain surgery, but you can rely on it in general, everyday situations. Keep a few things in mind. We live in the golden age of behavioural science and new discoveries are constantly being made. Sometimes it's out with the old, in with the new. No doubt we'll need to adjust things in future editions. More importantly, behavioural sciences

The Housefly Effect

work differently from the laws of physics. *The earth revolves around the sun, but not all the time?* Nonsense. But such statements are commonplace in behavioural sciences: people want both to belong *and* to stand out, like familiarity *and* novelty, love to be given a choice but hate choosing. Behaviour depends on the environment, as do housefly effects. So always give them a whirl in the laboratory. In the absence of a lab, find a small, dark corner, release the fly, and watch to see if something happens that's different from other dark corners without houseflies. Finally watch out for the **golden hammer effect**: becoming so excited about a solution that you think it's best for *every* problem. A housefly is no panacea. They *are* fascinating, useful, dangerous, funny and sometimes stunningly effective. So if you're sitting comfortably, then we'll begin.

What happens in Vegas also happens at home

Welcome to the Housefly Capital of the World: Las Vegas. This is where we'll introduce you to the seven housefly families, as in Las Vegas you find the cleverest operators of self-deception 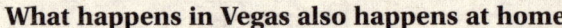, the best illusionists in the world. They're on stage, but there are even more of them behind the scenes in the casinos. Your brain tells you that you have a talent for the games, that you're often lucky, that you know when to stop, that you really won't be influenced by all those tricks. When you've read our first chapter, you'll know better. First you're obliged to exchange your money for chips. That's not for security, but because it's convenient, and with a chip like that you don't feel the payment pain associated with real money. All around you, you can see people striking it lucky, because the more prominently a slot machine is positioned, the more often it delivers a (modest) prize.* Once inside, your

---

* The story goes that funfair operators give away more big prizes in the morning for similar reasons. By the time you arrive, you see children going back and forth with enormous cuddly toys and you rate your chances of winning highly. But the

Introduction: The world's most famous fly

perception of time is instantly messed up to ensure that you continue playing and spending money. The architects have intentionally designed a maze where even after several days you still can't find the quickest route to the exit. The thick carpet slows your pace, and there's no clock in sight, other than the Swiss watches in the expensive shops where winners squander their gains. 'Daylight' comes exclusively from the painted blue sky above Paris, Venice or whichever other place in the world has been modelled to scale. Illuminated displays count down to yet another jackpot. The flickering lamps, the constant buzz of the machines, the small pay-outs along the way – they all give you the feeling that you could win if only you played a little bit longer.

Many a tourist flees Las Vegas after a few days, overstimulated and gasping for peace and nature. Tim sees this city as the ultimate natural phenomenon and takes great pleasure in a week's housefly safari (without gambling himself, please note). Those who stay longer or live there, however, often get into trouble. It's not only casinos; shops, petrol stations and even the airport are teeming with temptations to gamble. The result is hordes of local gambling addicts who keep telling themselves that the next game will make all the difference. These houseflies are like a biblical plague that no one can escape. Shouldn't the government protect that poor population against this?*

Well, that's America. Readers from elsewhere might feel that such excesses don't occur in their neck of the woods. We're a level-headed lot, so we tend not to deceive ourselves, and we certainly don't deceive others. Right? Hmm. Just go to a large furniture store, the kind where you have to assemble your bookcase or bed yourself. It's pretty difficult to walk through quickly, with

---

stakes have already been adjusted downwards. It's also said that fair operators spread this tale to attract more visitors in the quiet, early hours. In any case, the fair is swarming with flies.

* The government reaps 24 percent of the winnings in tax.

those confusing routes. And do you see daylight there? Yes, at the till, when they'd like you to hurry up... What about the supermarket, your favourite (web) shop or that nice restaurant? What happens in Las Vegas is just as common at home. Even in your daily life, there are all kinds of parties trying to influence you, and their most important accomplice is your own brain.

> The self-deception fly: ever present, never seen.

Musca deceptionis

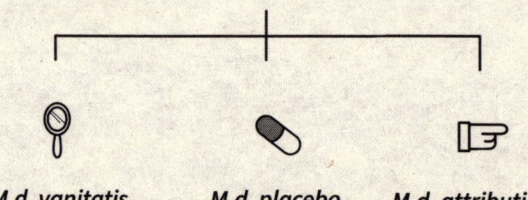

M.d. vanitatis *M.d. placebo* *M.d. attributionis*

Chapter 1

Our deceptive brain

Musca deceptionis or 'self-deception' fly

Subspecies: *M.d. vanitatis* (self-overestimation), *M.d. placebo*, *M.d. attributionis* (attribution error). This species of fly is barely visible to the human eye and virtually ineradicable. It crops up as a forerunner to other fly species: where *Musca deceptionis* emerges, others soon follow.

Application and management: in small numbers, just leave them to fly around, as they can also have positive consequences; in cases of sudden substantial growth, hold up a mirror. In a work environment it is recommended that *M.d. vanitatis* be cautiously encouraged.

Did you know that there are six different versions of *The Housefly Effect*, each with a different cover? Take a look what colour cover you have, because it says a lot about your personality. People who chose the orange edition are rather unique. On the one hand, they can be very extrovert and open. Orange is associated with expression and emotion. On the other hand, they can also be very introvert and 'live inside their own head'. The plain look of the cover appeals to this side of you. The combination of these two sides makes you really special. And it just so happens that for people like you we have an *extremely* promising investment opportunity!

Okay, of course you could tell something was up and you're quite right. There's actually only one cover in the shops.* But did you recognise something of yourself in the psychological profile we sketched? It's nothing to be ashamed of. It was inspired by a classic housefly effect known as the **Forer effect**. This is not so much a single effect as a series of statements that people think apply to them, but *not* to most other people. Soothsayers and palm readers were already using this trick far back in the last century, and in this day and age social media sites are full of posts along the lines of 'Like this if you're an introvert AND an extrovert!'†

---

* Of course we tested a number of variations on the cover design – different colours and different subtitles. The cover you're holding now was considered the most attractive.
† And, ladies, if a guy tells you, 'I believe there's a completely different side to you,'

Despite our explanation, you're still thinking: that may be so, but I happen to be one of those people who really are an introvert and an extrovert. Without wishing to sell your unique personality short, we human beings don't know ourselves as well as we think. The most effective houseflies make use of that. They hitch rides on the illusions, blind spots and shortcuts your brain has constructed in this area. So in order to understand those houseflies and to recognise them, you first need to view yourself differently.

Self-preservation versus self-knowledge

Are you a unique person who always makes conscious and well-considered choices based on facts? Or are your choices *also* the result of evolution, your genes, the situation and your environment? It's not one or the other; it's a combination. Music is a good analogy. Music arises when rhythm, melody, harmony and timbre come together. In the same way, behaviour arises from the confluence of biology, culture, circumstances and personality. The connection between them is therefore complicated. A lack of nutrients in the womb, for instance, can affect the function of a gene, which increases the chance of your reacting in a certain way in certain circumstances later in life. The implication is that people only have limited control over their behaviour. That's not the way it feels, though. War, exploitation, pollution, polarisation in society: sometimes the solution seems so simple. *If we all just stopped...* Unfortunately fMRI and EEG scans reveal all kinds of things inside the brain, but they don't show a reset button. However enlightened you may be, you can't turn your back on 300 million years of evolution. That's how deep-rooted matters such as tribalism, self-preservation and short-term thinking are. At best we can learn

---

he either has good instincts or he's been following very dodgy pickup artist courses (on which more later).

to be smarter in our management of the nice and not so nice sides of our behavioural repertoire. That process certainly doesn't always arise in a rational manner.

Classical economists worked on the assumption that human beings weigh up advantages and disadvantages to come to a decision. Looking at the choices people actually make, modern behavioural economists have come to a more nuanced view. Sure, your brain is constantly predicting and balancing the pros and cons of different options. When it comes to the crunch, though, the 'logic' used is of a different, primal kind. Do you leap straight into action without stopping to think? That may not make you management material in the modern business world, but on the steppe it might have saved the lives of your early ancestors. So you retain the impulse to make the snap decision that will ensure the survival of your genes here and now. That often runs counter to the demands of modern life, such as attentively comparing mortgage terms and choosing one that hurts slightly more now, but which you'll be glad of in thirty years' time. In short, those who consider themselves rational may be mistaken. But then the same goes for those who think they're sociable, loving or intuitive. The key lesson is not that humans are 'irrational', but that you can't trust introspection. We don't know ourselves nearly as well as we think.

The power of overestimating ourselves

Our lack of self-knowledge is revealed by the extent to which we overestimate ourselves. On balance, drivers consider themselves above average. Mathematically that's improbable, but apparently it feels that way, and this is something relatively objective: you know how many years you've built up on your no-claims bonus. For unmeasurable matters such as intuition and realism, people wildly overestimate themselves. Who doesn't have a high opinion of their own intuition or see their own viewpoints as realistic? We constantly overestimate ourselves. That might be a bit confrontational to read, but it helps us see ourselves for who we are. This is one of the things that make us human and, as we'll see later in this book, there are benefits to doing so. It only becomes problematic when it leads to poor choices.

A famous example of one such bad choice took place in Pittsburgh on 19 April 1995.[1] That day a man called McArthur Wheeler robbed two banks, not a clever thing to do in any case, but Wheeler decided to 'disguise' himself using lemon juice. That's to say, Wheeler knew lemon juice could be used as invisible ink (fun for kids: hold it over a radiator for a moment and it becomes visible), so he assumed he could also use it to make his face invisible to security cameras. According to the police, the man wasn't under the influence of drink or drugs. The story inspired professor of psychology David Dunning and student Justin Kruger to research what really lies behind such choices. This brought them to a much-vaunted housefly effect: the **Dunning–Kruger effect**.

This effect comes down to the following: those who know a little bit about a subject tend to substantially overestimate their own expertise. In part this is because they make decisions faster based on different memory processes.[2] You see it in every layer of society. Builders believe they could run the financial sector better and aren't shy about sharing this view on social media. The top manager is sure he can do his own renovation and ends up on *DIY SOS*. Not to mention the fashion model who after a few hours' research thinks she knows where medical science has gone wrong. The fascinating thing about this effect is that things also go awry higher up the learning curve. When you know more about a subject, you begin to see how much you still don't know. Every new piece of information adds to your ifs and buts: this doesn't always apply, further research is needed, that claim's not so robust... You end up drowning in nuance and become *so* reticent that you say nothing, leaving the first group, those who know little and are full of self-confidence, to gain the upper hand. Thus the naïve talk-show viewer is suddenly left listening to the soap actor's vision of a sustainable energy transition, honestly believing that his spur-of-the-moment opinion is as valuable as the advice of a scientific committee. Have you convinced yourself? The answer is surprisingly often yes.

The problem with overestimating yourself is that your intuition doesn't warn you when you're doing it. After all, it's intuition itself that has become derailed. That makes us vulnerable to tricks by illusionists and crooks; you can *feel* that you'll see which cup has the ball under it. Notably, it's often the highly educated who fall for scams,[3] making enormous bank transfers to fictitious internet lovers. They're extremely knowledgeable within their own subject area, and their overestimation of themselves leads them to assume that they will exhibit above average intelligence in other walks of life too: someone as clever as *me* would notice if it were fake. There's a good reason such scams are known as 'confidence tricks'; the scammer is playing with your (self-)confidence.

How should you deal with this? At the very least, never assume that you of all people are that exception who will win the game or receive that large sum from a Nigerian prince. If in doubt, ask the opinion of others, as we tend to overestimate one another rather less than ourselves.

Made for self-preservation, not self-knowledge

So your brain often plays tricks on you. But why? Is there something wrong with you? Your brain evolved to show you the most useful version of reality, which isn't the same as the most accurate one. Your brain makes decisions and has a press officer (the 'conscious' part) which defends those decisions against the outside world.[4] In any society you need certain traits to belong. A healthy dose of self-confidence, but also sufficient modesty. Reliability, of course, and, depending on your age, status, gender and culture, a certain propensity to be tough or caring. Such traits are difficult to fake in the long term: even the best actors sometimes fall out of their role. The smartest approach for your brain is therefore simply to allow your internal press officer to believe that you're put together a certain way. That maximises the chances of others believing it too.* This is the power of self-deception. The most dangerous demagogues and cult leaders have such sacrosanct faith in their story that they almost seem to bewitch others with it.

This is another way to look at the 'little voice' in your head, your internal monologue. One theory is that it arose as a preparation for possible conversations.[5†] If you secretly take one apple too many out of the communal basket, your brain will already be warming up for the discussion to follow: 'I'm extra hungry because I've worked so hard.' Gradually that little voice expanded to a long narrative about what you're like as a person, embellishing your strengths and placing your weaknesses in a positive light.‡ Such evolutionary explanations, however convincing, are hard to prove, but we like the idea that what we humans experience as our Self may have evolved as a trick to avoid nagging. One thing is certain: your consciousness doesn't know that much of how your brain works. And yes, that applies when the little voice in your head says, *I recognise all this in my boss, colleague, mother or brother... but not in*

---

* As an adman Tim often encounters this on a somewhat smaller scale. Halfway through the campaign he starts to crave this particular kind of ketchup or that brand of beer.

† It does seem to help: speakers are judged better by their audience when they are told to talk to themselves aloud in the second person. Imagine a footballer's internal monologue: 'So I'm telling myself, come on, Cristiano, you can do it, and then I shoot.'

‡ Some therapists help people consciously rewrite a mental story like this if it's getting in their way. That can be because it's *too* positive, or in fact very negative.

myself. So take that voice with a large pinch of salt. For enthusiasts there are entire meditative practices that can help you with this.

> **Try this at home**
>
> A party game. Give your housemates, colleagues or friends a pen and piece of paper. Ask them to estimate their own contribution, as a percentage, to a shared project: the housework, organising the annual office outing or how often someone is the designated driver. Depending on the size of the group, the sum of these numbers tends towards 150 percent. Essentially each person overestimates their contribution to the whole.
>
> Discuss it between you and after fifteen minutes or so, pose the same question again; most people will adjust their own contribution down a little, but the total will still be well over 100 percent.

Our insight into ourselves therefore leaves something to be desired and we systematically overestimate ourselves. But who is the beneficiary of that rose-tinted self-image? Ourselves or the outside world? Economists Joël van de Weele and Peter Schwardmann have researched this topic.[6] The question they sought to answer was: do we simply like our positive self-image, despite the fact that we are sometimes confronted with the harsh light of reality? Or do we engage in self-deception because overestimating ourselves is useful in the outside world?

Firstly the researchers showed that people generally overestimate themselves when it's convenient. Participants in the study had to do an intelligence test first and then indicate how they thought they'd scored. Like the drivers, the majority estimated themselves above average. They then received the results, but these were intentionally not entirely correct in some cases. Some participants received overly positive feedback: yes, you had a higher than average score! Those people were then better at convincing others of their intelligence than those with the same score who had received negative feedback. It even seemed as if people were implicitly aware of this, as those who knew they would subsequently have to convince another person of their cleverness estimated themselves somewhat higher in the first place.*

The key conclusion is that people overestimate themselves even more in social situations than in other contexts, and that it's useful too. Bluffing is something you do for others![7]

The law of Temptation Island

So the situation we find ourselves in affects our behaviour, but surely personality is the decisive factor? Many people think so. That certainly goes for the participants of one of our favourite scientific experiments: *Temptation Island*, a reality TV series in which couples are exposed to temptations. Beforehand the participants feel *sure* they'll stay faithful, because that's how they are, but once in the villa the world suddenly looks completely different. Heat, sun, alcohol, luxury… there are so many flies on that island. Virtually irresistible, it turns out. Context always wins out.

You may not be into reality TV full of dubious seducers and seductresses, but be honest: do you sometimes take risks on holiday that you wouldn't take at home? Well, you wouldn't be the only one. Tim once worked on government travel safety

---

* At presentations we're often asked whether these effects work differently for men and women. Generally the answer is no, but in this experiment, remarkably, it's yes. Men tend to overestimate themselves more in social situations. Subconscious strategic boasting is a specifically male trait, Eva concludes with some satisfaction. Tim is keen to add that he's long known this, because he's great at this sort of thing.

campaigns. They were supposed to dissuade citizens who obediently follow the Highway Code at home from getting behind the wheel of their holiday rental cars while drunk. Different context, different behaviour. What else is new? Of course you behave differently in the gym from in church, with your partner as opposed to with your boss, in the school playground compared with in a nightclub. Everyone knows that, yet we tend to keep on underestimating the influence of the situation.

The same goes for healthy resolutions, such as stopping smoking, drinking less or exercising more. People tend to rely on willpower, on personality alone, but if you recognise the influence of circumstances, you'll know that it can be *much* more effective to change those. Free will may in fact mean the freedom to influence your environment. You could avoid having crisps in the house, for instance, instead of trying to resist them with an iron will. Those genuinely wishing to stay faithful to their partners will travel as a couple to a nice hotel. It may not be a luxury villa, but at least it's an environment conducive to quality couple time.

The player got played?

After the 2016 American elections there was a great deal of fuss about the company Cambridge Analytica, which was thought to have used illegally gathered Facebook data to target people, based on their psychological characteristics. Everyone was then shown precisely the reason for voting for Trump that best fitted their profile. Anxious personalities were told, 'Don't let America down!' Open personalities received 'Discover America's future!' Meanwhile, former employees have taken to the lecture circuit to explain how it's done. The company uses

Facebook data to divide people according to the 'Big 5' personality traits model, one of the few classifications that many psychologists believe holds water.[8] With a few thousand users' likes, the system would be better at predicting their psychological test result than their own partner. It would then send them adverts specifically targeted at them. Scientists were curious whether those claims stood up. And yes, they saw that an advert that fitted a person's psychological profile really did increase their intention to vote for a particular candidate.[9]

There are doubts as to how much this affects actual behaviour. Trump's social media expert Brad Parscale, in any case, distanced himself from these practices in subsequent elections, not because they were unethical (note, this is Trump's social media expert we're talking about), but because he felt that they weren't effective enough. During the 2021 Dutch elections, the conservative party, the CDA, poured limitless resources into social media advertising and really went for it, but the intended effect eluded them. Perhaps Cambridge Analytica doesn't so much fool voters as it does its own unscrupulous clients.

You see what suits you

In one case people do see the influence of circumstances very clearly: when they've done something wrong. Anyone who has made a mistake, broken someone's trust, failed to keep a promise, suddenly has no trouble whatsoever recognising the influence of circumstances. In fact, the circumstances are the standard excuse:

The Housefly Effect

'This isn't who I really am, I got caught up in it all.' This is a familiar pattern: the fundamental attribution error.

Ask a successful entrepreneur about the secret of his success and he will generally say something like, 'I'm a naturally hard worker.' So it's their personality that determines their behaviour! But when the same person has to apologise for a slip, do they say, 'I'm naturally the kind of person who unreasonably insists on getting his own way'? No, then the answer is usually more along these lines: 'I was going through a difficult period and did things in the moment that I would never normally do.' The outside world, funnily enough, sees things precisely the other way around. 'He's had a lot of luck in his career, but now he's revealed his true colours.' If *you* run a red light, it's a one-off emergency measure because, for reasons completely beyond your control, you're late for a very important appointment. But what are your thoughts on a stranger you see driving through a red light for no apparent reason? This **fundamental attribution error** is hard to avoid, but at least you now know not to take life lessons from the autobiographies of successful people too seriously. And that you sometimes have to bite your tongue before you offer an extremely one-sided explanation for your success or failure.

Well, we aren't as clever as we think, don't listen to feedback and ascribe strokes of luck to our own talent. But at least we're honest about it, right? Alas, your integrity is also determined by the situation. In a podcast[10] Dan Ariely, one of the most prominent researchers on self-deception, gives an example of how honesty and self-deception are points on a slippery slope:

> 'I have a disability, but it's not particularly severe. I was standing with a friend in a long queue for the check-in desk and asked him to get me a wheelchair. It wasn't strictly necessary, but we were soon checked in. Okay, I cheated. I was sitting there in that wheelchair, so my friend had to push me to my place and to the

> toilet. But I was sitting in seat D37 or thereabouts, so I didn't drink anything the entire flight. Afterwards, completely in character and extremely frustrated, I complained to the airline that it's degrading how they treat people in wheelchairs.'

Ariely doesn't tell this rather cringeworthy anecdote just to entertain. He uses it to reveal the core of self-deception: that lying, like boasting, works best when you believe it yourself. This brings him to a slippery slope. He can 'sell' this deception to his self-image because he really is slightly disabled. In doing so, he suggests that your self-image, and whether you're capable of maintaining it, is a determining factor in how you behave. And here they are again, those buzzing flies. People straightforwardly avoid situations where a donation is requested. If there's someone with a collection bucket outside the supermarket, everyone simply walks past. But in an experiment, when people saw that the collector made eye contact and spoke to passers-by, almost one in three took a different exit.[11] You don't like to see yourself as someone who says no to a good cause.

Does this ring a bell? Or do you not really believe that the environment and your self-image are crucial to your behaviour? Fair enough – people may actively[12] choose to deceive themselves.[13]*

The housefly that works without doing anything

There are all sorts of strange things for sale on Amazon, but our favourite is the product Zeebo. Its slogan: 'Pure honest placebo for immediate effect.' These are authentic placebo pills, available without prescription, for 'symptom relief, concentration, clarity, energy, calm.' Should you doubt their efficacy, check out satisfied

---

* Still here? Did you know that clever people are even better at manipulating themselves?

The Housefly Effect

customer Oshe, who gives the product four stars and a glowing review: 'Really good placebo pills [...] does what it's supposed to do.'

Placebos are a special category of self-deception houseflies. You'll be familiar with them from the medical world, where they're primarily used in tests to compare the effect of real medicine with the reaction to a fake pill. You probably also know that placebos can sometimes be beneficial. The body anticipates the effect so well that patients really do experience less pain or more energy. The placebo effect has been around for some time. Thomas Jefferson wrote in 1807 that a doctor friend had had great success with drops of coloured water. During World War II medics used placebos when the real medicines ran out, sometimes to astonishing effect.

Obviously an amputated leg won't suddenly grow back after taking a dummy pill, but pain, stress and listlessness can genuinely be alleviated. There are various ways of creating an even more effective placebo: make it big or expensive, get people to rub it in carefully, inject it or even apply it via a surgical non-intervention. Cut open, sew up and done. A white placebo works better for headaches, a red one gives patients more energy. People also report greater benefits when there are more side effects listed in the information leaflet. The downside is the **nocebo effect**, which arises when people receive a placebo and experience the side effects of the real medicine. In fact, even if people know they're receiving a placebo, they still experience better results than those who don't take anything. How meta can you get? Your brain anticipates a placebo effect and creates that experience!

Now we're not expecting you to rush to Amazon and buy a box of Zeebo. Still, there's a good chance you experience placebo effects in your daily life, without even thinking about it. Imagine the following scenario. Two colleagues are together in the office. One feels a bit chilly and turns the thermostat up, after which the other feels a little on the warm side. There's some further fiddling with the settings and irritated words are exchanged, but eventually they arrive at a temperature they both find acceptable: the ideal working climate. 'HANDS OFF!' they write on a Post-it note. Do you have colleagues like this, or do you do this yourself? Never take that thermostat box off the wall, because there may be nothing behind it. You're the 'victim' of a placebo button. They're more common than you might think. In America journalists asked air-conditioning professionals if they had ever installed placebo buttons: of the seventy-one who responded, fifty said yes.* And what about the 'close door' button in the lift: does it really close the door? Or would it have closed anyway? What about pedestrian crossings? The city of New York, for example, has 3,250 buttons on lights at pedestrian crossings, 2,500 of which do absolutely nothing. At least from a technical point of view. What they do achieve is to give people the feeling that they have some influence on their waiting time at the stop light – making them less likely to recklessly throw themselves under a taxi.

Because that's the remarkable thing about this category of housefly effects: placebos don't do anything, but they do work.†

> **A noticeable effect**
>
> Not technically a placebo, but this is a related phenomenon: the houseflies that have no effect but give the impression of having one. In his memoir, advertising legend Jerry Della Femina recalls an innovative product that failed: an antibacterial facial cleanser that didn't sting. After a while

---

* We read this in *The New York Times*, but their source is far more fun: *The Air Conditioning, Heating and Refrigeration News*, 2003. You're a regular reader too, right?
† Most people are sensitive to placebos, to varying degrees. It remains unclear exactly what causes the variation.

it became clear that users actually welcomed the stinging sensation on their skin: they wanted to feel that it was doing something. Nowadays product developers routinely take this into account. For instance they make toothpaste tingle in your mouth more than is necessary, and lots of cough syrup tastes worse than required so it seems medicinal. A famous example in marketing circles is that Coca-Cola Light, ever popular with female customers, is intentionally given a more dilute flavour than its manlier counterpart Coca-Cola Zero. Consumer panels revealed that women like to be able to taste the fact that they have renounced sugar and are on the right track. In the technological world there's less attention to such effects. For instance, Microsoft removed the save button from Word for the web, because any changes are saved automatically. In doing so, however, they forgot the emotional contribution of that button: reassurance and a sense of satisfaction in getting something done.

You feel better in a Peugeot

Brands are in some sense the ultimate placebos. When you get people to taste blind, the best-selling cola turns out not to be judged the tastiest.* Show the brand and suddenly people honestly prefer the number one. Lager drinkers often don't even recognise their favourite brand in blind tests. A special category here is

---

* Such tests can also be influenced by sneaky houseflies. One cola is tastier served ice-cold, another at room temperature, and something that's lovely for a single sip may be disgusting after five.

high-end audio. Twenty-four-carat-gold plugs, speaker cables that cost more than a new family car. Enthusiasts swear that they can hear a big difference as soon as anything changes. We recently heard on the grapevine of someone whose music no longer sounded good after the switch to green energy! You can feel it coming: blind tests find little or no evidence for this. The cheap cable from the discount basket near the till sounds just as good.*
Yet enthusiasts experience immense enjoyment outside these tests, thanks to their extremely expensive stereo systems. A pricey housefly, but hey, if you can afford it and enjoy it, why not? But if we were you, we wouldn't take out a loan for it. If in doubt, do a blind test.

Besides avoiding placebo effects, you can also use them in your daily life. That certainly doesn't require a trip to the doctor. Take Michelin-starred chefs, for example, because they have an excellent understanding of this housefly. From the stylish reception area to the story about the Tibetan monastery that inspired some finicky molecular process and, of course, the star that the restaurant so proudly displays: before you've tasted a single bite, your brain already knows it. This is going to involve refined, layered, surprising flavours. In the battle for the stars, chefs go ever further. How about headphones to play you precisely the right soundtrack for your poached oyster? Of course people like you don't fall for tricks like that. But that oyster was heavenly! So if you serve your guests cheap plonk from a chic bottle, they will genuinely taste fine wine.† Brain research shows that the

---

* About that discount basket: housefly alert! This is an immensely effective trick based on the principle that presenting things in a big pile helps them to sell. When you place things in a heap or basket, people instantly believe they're cheap. That basket implies: everything must go, discount bucket, we're earning so little from this that we couldn't even afford a normal shelf. Often in actual fact the price is no lower than normal.
† See also the documentary *Sour Grapes*, in which millionaires cheerfully spend thousands of dollars on supermarket wines.

idea that wine is expensive really does affect the degree of enjoyment.[14] This effect extends beyond 'talking yourself into it'; the stimulus is fake, but the experience is authentic. So put your toddler's carrots in colourful fast-food packaging and she really will find them tastier.

What you don't know...

A nice scientific term for self-deception is 'strategic ignorance'. Do people consciously turn a blind eye to undesirable information? In order to find out, scientists developed a simple experiment. Participants were offered a meal and allowed to choose whether they wanted to see how many calories it contained. The result: as many as 46 percent left the envelope with that information closed. They apparently preferred to savour their food without feeling guilty. And self-deception – sorry, strategic ignorance – doesn't stop there. When the scientists asked (other) people what they would do in this case, only 19 percent said they would leave the envelope untouched. So we even deceive ourselves as to the extent to which we deceive ourselves.[15]

(By the way, have you seen the documentary *Cowspiracy*, about the shocking land and water usage involved in meat consumption? It's very convincing – you'll never want meat again after watching it. The link is below).[16]*

---

* No one who eats meat is likely to read this. The information leads to awkward questions of conscience, which people prefer to avoid. For the brave and the vegans: cowspiracy.com.

Our deceptive brain

Your brain as an accomplice

You're onto the fact that your brain often plays tricks on you. Does this mean you won't fall for it any more? Have you now attained a higher state of consciousness?

Sadly, being aware of a glitch in your brain won't automatically enable you to avoid it. The best illustration of this is optical illusions. However often you say to yourself that the lines in the next image are the same length, you keep on seeing them differently. This realisation is fundamental to the rest of this book, because it's precisely this automatic, inevitable self-deception that makes your brain sensitive to housefly effects.

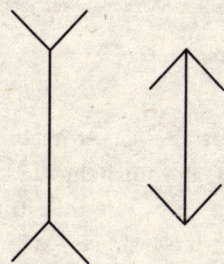

Yes, you *know* they're the same length,
but do you actually see it that way?

Try this at home

Do your children leave food on their plates? Use the **Delboeuf illusion**. Instead of giving them a little children's plate, give them the biggest plate you have in the house. The same portion of food then looks a good deal more manageable. If you double the size of the plate, 41 percent more gets eaten.[17] The opposite works too: that's why all-you-can-eat restaurants have those silly little plates.

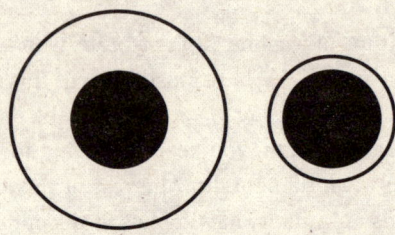

The Delboeuf illusion. The black circles on the left and right are the same size, yet the portion on the left looks considerably more manageable.

Your very own brain is the secret accomplice of all kinds of parties who wish to steer your behaviour in some way. Again, optical illusions help us illustrate this. Think of traffic. How do you get people to drive more slowly? With signs, fines, cameras and campaigns? That's one way of doing things. Or you could use optical narrowing. Your brain fools you into thinking the road is narrower. It's not, but you slow down just in case. The same happens with a 3D zebra crossing, which, owing to clever paintwork, looks like it's hovering above the road. Your brain shows you an obstacle, your foot goes to the brake. This dirty trick is also applied in hospitality. The same quantity of drink looks much more generous in a narrower glass with a thicker bottom. Your brain sees a fuller glass and accepts that it costs more.

It follows from this that you can also deploy your brain as an accomplice in your own plans: buy smaller plates and you really will eat less. For the most cunning houseflies of this variety you need to go to Walt Disney World. Some buildings here have half floors to create a targeted false perspective, so that the street appears longer and more imposing than it really is, culminating in that magical castle. For anyone who has driven some distance, queued in the scorching sun and spent a fortune on tickets, that view makes them feel they've reached the Promised Land: it was all worth it! You may have been manipulated by that clever company, but your own brain was complicit at the very least.

You slow down more readily for a 'floating' zebra crossing than for a sign.

Try this at home

Fill in the gaps in the words below.

DEER   FINGERS

H_ND   H_ND

When you fill in the examples above, do you read HIND followed by HAND? The context determines your expectation, your brain fills in the rest. In other words, 'deer' and 'fingers' steered you in a particular mental direction, an example of **priming**.

Priming alert!

When attending a drinks reception, never hold a cold drink in your right hand! Those who offer a warm handshake are perceived as warmer people. Print your CV on heavy paper and the recruitment committee will see you as a more serious candidate. When a Mars landing appears in the news, more Mars bars are sold. These are all appealing examples, of course. But beware, priming research is not uncontroversial. Some notable experiments were done with very few participants and, when repeated, they sometimes give different results. It seems fair to say that the researchers jumped to conclusions. The stories about subliminal advertising (involving brief hidden messages in films to make viewers rush for the popcorn) may well leave you reeling. The original tests certainly led to massive societal outcry: this kind of brainwashing had to be banned. A few years later, however, it emerged that those tests had been faked, a scam to sell that type of advert. But before you breathe a sigh of relief: in 2006 researchers at Utrecht University tried it out for real,[18] with some genuine success – in a laboratory setting – influencing behaviour with quick, flashing images. A British attempt to replicate this outside the lab, however, came to nothing. In short, priming exists, but we don't yet understand enough about precisely how and when it works. For now, therefore, we'd say, don't attach overly weighty conclusions to such studies.

But in this chapter you *have* discovered that your brain evolved to deceive you. In part that's down to 'shortcuts'; your brain draws conclusions that often apply, but not always (think of the optical illusions). A big part of self-deception is down to the press officer in your brain, who often causes you to overestimate yourself: think of all those above-average drivers, of the Forer effect and the Dunning–Kruger effect. You've seen how you tell yourself that you deserve your success, whereas you blame your failures on circumstances, and how you perceive the precise opposite when it comes to others: the fundamental attribution error. You've discovered that placebos occur not only in medical experiments but also in your work, in the lift and at the dining table. And you've read how organisations and companies take advantage of all that, enlisting your deceptive brain as an accomplice.

Now you may be looking around you suspiciously and swiping at the imaginary flies circling around your head. They're everywhere! But relax, sometimes you can avoid them. Other times you can even use them to your advantage – preferably in a responsible manner. And if those tactics don't work, you can at least recognise them and smile to yourself. In the next chapter we'll tell you how to go about doing all that. Trust us. We'd never deceive you, right?

The lazy fly takes the path of least resistance.

Musca inertiae

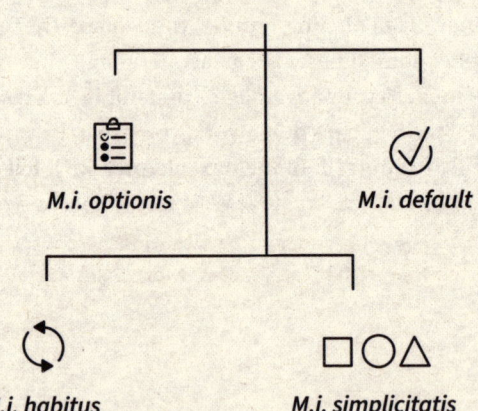

M.i. optionis

M.i. default

M.i. habitus

M.i. simplicitatis

Chapter 2
The power of convenience

Musca inertiae or 'lazy fly'

Subspecies: *M.i. optionis* (choice effects), *M.i. default* (default option), *M.i. habitus* (habit), *M.i. simplicitatis* (simplicity).

An ostensibly ordinary and therefore often overlooked fly. In reality, a formidable foe, the natural enemy of desirable behaviour and good intentions. Can be seen swarming round the heads of opportunistic politicians, frequently found in supermarkets, while also increasingly common in the public sector. Impossible to eradicate but easy enough to avoid with some attention. Conversely, *Musca inertiae* can be deployed in combatting undesirable situations, from making unhealthy choices to getting into arrears. Motto: I'm not a bug, I'm a feature.

In 2014, an extraordinary start-up entered the market. Washboard was aimed at people who use laundrettes and need coins for this. Of course, you can save up your coppers or exchange notes at a bank or change machine, but that's all a bit of a faff. Washboard responded to this gap in our increasingly cash-free society with a useful subscription service, charging a mere 27 dollars a month for a whopping 80 quarters! Yup, that amounts to 20 dollars. Washboard didn't last very long. But not for a lack of customers. The company was beset by financial and legal issues. (We like to think it was something to do with money laundering. He he!) But there was one thing the Washboard founders certainly understood: people are prepared to fork out good money to avoid a bit of effort. And that's a potent housefly effect.

Welcome to the path of least resistance

'Start with why' is a well-known approach within marketing. In this chapter, we'd like to turn that on its head. If you're asking people to do something that to all intents and purposes is enjoyable, fun, good, sensible and beneficial for them to do, then why are they not already doing it? So 'start with why not'. The answer may lie in deep-rooted psychological resistance, but often it's more superficial: what you're asking people to do is simply too much hassle. Wherever possible, the brain tries to avoid effort, be it physical exertion (getting small change, posting a receipt, cycling into town) or something as minor as bending over or standing on tiptoe. Marketers in Reykjavik managed to double the market share of a crisp brand in a test store, which amounts to a major feat in the world of marketing. How, I hear you ask. Was it a particularly creative campaign? A clever strategy that changed the way people think about crisps? Nothing of the sort. They moved the bags from somewhere lower down up to the middle shelf: easily visible and within reach. Businesses like to think of their regular buyers as loyal fans but, if you're having to bend down for that familiar packaging, you're more likely to put a rival brand in your trolley. The brain will opt for the path of least resistance.

It goes without saying that companies are only too happy to capitalise on this and make it easy for you to select their product. Behind the scenes of your local supermarket, producers are locked in intense negotiations, trying to get their goods into the store, in a high-traffic aisle, all nicely laid out on a prominent shelf and ideally at eye level, because 'eye level is buy level'. Packaging is designed so it's easy to pick up (like plastic fruit punnets with a handle) and leaves little or no doubt about the contents. Major manufacturers develop entire 'shelf designs' in an attempt to persuade retail chains of the best possible layout for the beer or instant soup sections – with their brands in a starring role, of course. As well as any form of physical discomfort, these businesses like to remove all mental effort. And doubt is eliminated with good brand recognition, a generous sprinkling of reassuring certifications and all manner of guarantees.

Until recently, the non-commercial arena looked completely different. For many public bodies, the target group's convenience was the least of their concerns. The reasons for this are manifold, but *housefly blindness* is one of them. Organisations often fail to recognise that something small can have a huge effect. Take the little extra effort asked of people to pay a fine on time. If that penalty is paid late, the payer will go further into arrears and receive even more difficult paperwork to fill in. The long-term consequences can be disastrous and lead to spiralling debt. Governments have resigned over smaller scandals. Luckily, we're now seeing a shift. In the past decade the buzzword in councils and other government circles has been *nudge*, a term introduced by Richard Thaler in what has since become a bestseller.[1] Nudging can be defined as gently encouraging or persuading someone to do something by making it the easy, obvious and – where possible – fun option. For instance, healthy foods can be placed front and centre in the company canteen, the stairs decorated with cool stickers that indicate how many calories you're burning with each step or the entire staircase transformed into a joyful piano that plays music as you climb it. Likewise, forms can be partially filled in and a handy VAT reminder added to the app. And, by dropping subtle hints to the effect that others in the neighbourhood have already paid their bill, you can appeal to people's latent sense of wanting to be part of the group.*

A lot can be said about the ethics and efficacy of nudging – we'll come back to that at the end of this book – but one thing is clear: if you can make something easier, then that means it's unnecessarily difficult right now. In a nod to nudging, the same Richard Thaler calls this *sludging*. Where a nudge seeks to make the desired behaviour easy, fun and the obvious choice, a *sludge* does the opposite, forcing the target group to metaphorically wade through a thick, impenetrable soup of 'sludge' to reach their destination. Again, this is something we see in retail. *Cashback* is a common type of offer. The sign says *£25 OFF!* but the small print informs you that you have to pay full whack now before claiming back those £25 at home. No trouble at all, you'd think; easy money. Yet most consumers

---

* That said, we like to steer clear of the trend of referring to everything that's approached from a behavioural perspective as 'nudging'. A nudge is a change in the choice architecture, one that stimulates a specific type of behaviour, not a brochure, however clever its illustrations.

never claim their cash back, making this one of the most lucrative promotions for manufacturers. Some marketing books suggest the figure is as high as 40 percent! People leave it too late, which is also why gift cards and loyalty points programmes are such big money spinners. But it goes without saying that marketing people like to make the process difficult. It explains why the terms and conditions are brimming with houseflies. You can't claim your cash back until two months after your purchase, and to do so you'll need both your original receipt and the barcode on the packaging. Or else – and it takes some cheek to ask for this – the sticker on the back of the television that's been mounted on the wall for the past two months. Each little fly leads to a decrease in the percentage of people who cross the finishing line – and an increase in profits for the manufacturer, who nets the extra revenue from this great offer at a fraction of the cost.

Marketers are paid to generate sludge, but the public sector is, unintentionally, the biggest sludge producer of all. 'That's not my department', 'That's only done on Mondays', 'You need a different form' and 'Sorry, madam, I didn't make the rules'. In the United States people sometimes have to queue for hours to register to vote, while anyone wanting to cancel a rail season ticket in the Netherlands has to press the 'collect a prepaid ticket' button – not on a website, but at an actual station. But progress is possible, even in the public sector: after a recent scandal involving complicated paperwork, the Dutch government introduced a '*doenvermogentoets*' or 'capacity-to-act test', stipulating that regulations should be designed so that people can not only understand them but also act on them, regardless of whether they have crushing debts or hungry children or simply happen to be juggling a lot of other things.

Maybe you're thinking that this particular housefly, *Musca inertiae*, mainly buzzes around trivial things. If you *really* want something, you won't be put off by a bit of effort, right? That's true, up to a point. The most inspirational biographies are about people who face opposition and setbacks but, thanks to herculean efforts, eventually achieve their goal. But that's usually not a discount on an electric toothbrush. Effort and exertion can play a greater role in matters of life and death than you think. In the UK, for example, the number of suicides dropped sharply when manufacturers switched from family-sized containers of paracetamol to smaller blister packs and imposed a limit on how many a customer could buy. This made it impossible for anyone to neck a bottle of pills in a moment of despair. Of course, overdosing on painkillers is not the only method used by people with suicidal tendencies, but this 'sludge' did save many lives.

So sludging can be a positive thing. And the great news is that you can create sludge for yourself, from the comfort of your own home! In the US, where consumers have been known to make impulse buys on credit, people sometimes actually freeze their credit card in a block of ice. At the very least, it gives them a literal cooling-off period before committing to that purchase. This ice block is an effective visualisation of the asymmetry of sludge: just as it's usually easier to take out a subscription than to cancel it, a credit card is in the freezer in no time at all but that tub of frozen water will take much longer to melt. It goes to show that it *really* matters whether something is made easy or not.

Our limited brain

Are people really that lazy? That's one way of putting it. Or as some would say: 'It's not a bug, it's a feature.' Avoiding (mental) effort is a clever and efficient strategy deployed by your brain.

Over your head

Imagine scenario 1: a fashion designer opens a boutique. He hires a grand old building and decides to make use of the high ceilings by stylishly displaying all garments five metres in the air. Do you think he'll sell a lot? Of course not. People don't buy things they can't physically reach.

Here's scenario 2: to encourage entrepreneurs to work more sustainably, a local council communications officer sends out an ingenious 78-slide PowerPoint presentation, chock-full of facts and figures, charts and graphs, technical specifications, interviews with experts, best practices and whatnot. That'll get their attention! What do these two scenarios have in common? The communications officer is making the exact same mistake as the fashion designer. Both fail to take the *physicality* of their target audience into account. People aren't 16 feet tall, nor do they have a huge brain that's capable of processing endless quantities of complex data. Both the outfits and the information are way over people's heads.

Of course you know your brain has its limits, but this cap on your thinking power probably feels a little less unequivocal than that on stature. That's not surprising. We tend to see what's going on inside our heads as intangible – and so perhaps as malleable too. 'Anything is possible, if only you want it!' But alas, contrary to popular belief, you don't use just a percentage, but the full 100 percent of your brain. Your skull contains nothing but around three pounds of grey matter and is an organ that, like your arms and legs, has physical limitations. Your brain comprises 2 percent of your body weight but uses 20 percent of your oxygen supply and calorie intake (the latter is roughly the equivalent of a greasy hamburger a day).*

Your brain has to utilise that energy as well as possible as it guides you through life. This means being efficient in making dizzying numbers of decisions, sometimes estimated at around 35,000 a day. (We'd love to know who tallied them all up.) Straightening your specs, typing a word or two, taking a sip of water... we do something nearly every second and for the brain to manage this, it has to process information. When this calls for making calculations, weighing up facts or coming up with clever approaches, the prefrontal cortex plays a starring role. That complicates matters, because of its relatively limited capacity. Having evolved some 100 million years later, it's a little younger than other structures in the brain, which means it's less fully developed and therefore less efficient. Comparatively, this region takes up a lot of space but works nowhere near as fast as, say, those parts that make you sneeze or jump when startled.†

Nobel Prize winner Daniel Kahneman introduced an apt analogy for the way our brain functions: 'Thinking is to humans as swimming is to cats; they can do it, but they'd prefer not to.' Kahneman identifies two modes of thought: a rational, measured little voice in the back of your head, and a rapid, automatic system. A surprising number of choices are made using this second approach, on autopilot. Sometimes almost literally, for instance when you cycle somewhere and on arrival can't remember what route you took to get there. While the voice inside your head – the slow mode – was making a lot of noise, the automatic system got you to pedal, steer, brake, turn corners and hopefully signal and check your surroundings every now and then. It's often said that fast thinking is responsible for anywhere between 95 and

---

* Maybe we should have called this book *Think Yourself Slim*. We reckon it would have sold better.

† Or, since coronavirus days, make you jump when somebody sneezes.

99 percent of our decisions. While not giving percentages, Kahneman himself agrees that a vast number of our actions are automatic. And because of the speed with which this happens, we often find ourselves already doing something before we give it any conscious attention. It's only after the event that the press officer steps in to provide a plausible explanation – if deliberate thought comes into the picture at all.

Houseflies have a tendency to get you to do things on autopilot. Remember that fly in the toilet bowl? Or how about this: in January 2021 a mob of Trump supporters stormed the Capitol, clashing with security staff, smashing windows and vandalising property. One particular image stood out. Once inside, the rioters dutifully followed the route marked by those neat little posts with velvet ropes. On autopilot. 'It' must be in that direction. The Amsterdam-based bicycle manufacturer VanMoof has taken advantage of this kind of involuntary behaviour with an ingenious hack. The company ships its bikes around the globe but found that they'd often get damaged in transit. As a courier you're bound to think: oh, a bike, it can take a knock or two. FRAGILE! stickers had little or no effect and the cost of returning the (pricey) bikes was sky-rocketing. So the clever clogs at VanMoof had the image of a smart TV printed on their flat boxes, and guess what? Breakage was reduced by 70 to 80 percent. This is the same automatic system that supermarkets target when they aim a warm yellow spotlight at their bananas, place juices in the chiller cabinet that are perfectly fine unrefrigerated or pump the smell of fresh bread into the store using a machine called a Smellitzer. The products practically fly into your basket, on autopilot.

Lessons we can learn from The Donald (like it or not)

Now you may be wondering whether all this applies with equal force to those with a university education, blue personality types,

Sagittarii or even women (we actually get asked this question from time to time). That's to say, you want to know whether you, or your social group, are the exception to the rule and make more informed decisions? No. In this area there's precious little difference between healthy brains. If anything, anyone taking decisions on the strength of carefully considered facts would need a much bigger brain. And a gigantic head. Given that this would make a healthy, full-term pregnancy impossible (we're already born early and helpless because of our large skulls), we'll just have to wait for Elon Musk to design an AI plug-in for our minds. Until then, your brain can't possibly weigh up all the available information for each individual decision.* Google 'best vacuum cleaner' and you'll get millions of results. Herbert Simon, one of the founding fathers of artificial intelligence, said as much 80 years ago: 'A wealth of information creates a scarcity of attention.'[2] In other words: attempts to persuade someone with a lot of detailed facts and figures will often misfire.

It's what gives simplicity its powerful housefly effect, and also explains the title of a classic book on web design: *Don't Make Me Think*.[3] Your brain has a preference for things that are easy to process, for *cognitive fluency*. When something is clear and super-easy to understand, it gives you a good feeling. Your hard-working prefrontal cortex doesn't have to worry about it! This fly is a dangerous creature, because style and substance are two entirely separate matters. And when you're not actively thinking about something, you are, by definition, less critical. It's the reason American spin doctors encourage their candidates to keep things as simple as possible. But occasionally some nuance will slip through. This was Hillary Clinton's stance on immigration in 2016:

---

* That's why Barack Obama always wore the same suit – it was one less decision to make.

The power of convenience

> *I believe that when we have millions of hard-working immigrants contributing to our economy, it would be self-defeating and inhumane to try to kick them out. Comprehensive immigration reform will grow our economy and keep families together, and it's the right thing to do.*

Nothing wrong with this position. But it does require a bit of prefrontal activity.* Her opponent took a different approach:

> BUILD A WALL.

It doesn't get simpler than that. Who knows, maybe Clinton could have changed the course of history had she just said:

> *Keep families together.*

But would she have been willing to? Those keen to move people often face the diabolical dilemma of having to 'sacrifice' subtlety. 'Man hungry? Ding-dong pizza!' sums up pizza delivery in the simplest of terms. Tim is still envious of the slogan. That said, there will have been some lingering regret at company headquarters that the fresh ingredients, crispy crust and wealth of vegetarian options didn't get a mention. And what's true of fast food applies all the more to environmental issues, prudent economic policy and vital medical research. Because the people working in these areas are often resistant to (over)simplification, their messages tend to get lost in nuance,[4]† giving (opposing) parties who aren't that bothered about facts a clear advantage. Just think of TV

---

* In case you scanned or skipped the quote: a fine piece of energy management by that brain of yours.
† It explains why the titles of scientific articles tend to be impenetrably long. But even scientists have lazy brains and are more likely to cite articles with shorter titles.

shopping channels making bold claims like, 'Developed for space travel, so it's guaranteed to make *your* life better!' Many an unwary viewer will fall for it. This housefly effect is known as **because validation**. The fact that an argument is given at all is enough for the busy brain. Why? Because. 'Can I use the photocopier first? I have some copying to do.' A pretty nonsensical addition, if ever there was one, and certainly not a convincing argument for jumping the queue. But that doesn't stop a superfluous reason working like a housefly, as it's much more effective than 'Mind if I go first?' without a rationale.[5*] Sneaky? Effective? Yes and yes. And remember: It's going to be a beautiful summer, so go out and buy an extra copy of *The Housefly Effect*!

The trash can wind meter and other ways of simplifying things

Let's face it: lots of things simply *aren't* that simple. But luckily almost everything can be simplified a little.

Let's go over to Eva and Gerd now with a look at the weather

Eva's first research project looked at how well people understand something as straightforward as the weather forecast. What do you think 'a 23 percent chance of rain tomorrow' means?

---

* Only 60 percent got to go first without a motivation, compared to 91 percent with a nonsense reason. The figure was barely any higher with a better rationale ('I'm in a rush'): 92 percent.

The power of convenience

> A. There will be at least one drop of rain 23 percent of the time tomorrow.
>
> B. 23 percent of the forecast area will see at least one drop of rain tomorrow.
>
> C. 23 percent of days like tomorrow will see at least one drop of rain.
>
> In collaboration with the guru of risk literacy, Gerd Gigerenzer, and a group of other researchers, Eva looked at how the public in various countries interpret this probability. In Milan it was understood to mean: 23 percent of the region will get wet (perhaps because the city is in a mountainous area with huge regional differences). New Yorkers fared better with most people thinking that 23 percent of days like tomorrow would see precipitation. And the Dutch? A majority thought it would be raining 23 percent of the time. One person explained to Eva: 'It's not about duration, it's obviously about the quantity of rain.'[6]

Some ingenious forecasts in the US use a 'trash can wind meter', with the meteorologist telling you whether tomorrow's gusts will knock over your wheelie bin, propel it into your neighbour's garden or into the street or whether it will go missing altogether. It's a lot easier to understand than 'a southeasterly wind, force seven'. Numbers don't tell you what you really want to know when you watch the weather report. The same is true for scales. Only an anaesthetist or hot-air balloonist wants to know your *exact* weight. Most people just wonder whether their diet is working or what toll their fun weekend has taken. The answer to these questions isn't 71.8 kilos and that makes it difficult to act accordingly. If anything, having such precise knowledge can be counterproductive, as many people become either demoralised or overexcited by tiny fluctuations. This inspired US scientists to develop numberless scales that show a rising or falling line over a two-week period. It really can be that simple. Even when things can't be simplified, you can get them to look less complicated.

The brain is a prediction machine that responds not to *actual* but to estimated effort. That's why ads are always telling you how incredibly easy it is to become a member, take part in something or install your own kitchen – usually followed by a neat list of bullet points. Split a challenging task into separate stages or steps and it will instantly appear much easier. It's this, *chunking*, that gives a good manual its distinct power, in the same way that a phased plan is the best way of motivating people in an organisation.

Simply complex

This housefly can also be found in the weirdly fascinating guise of **complexity bias**. Sometimes our brain finds it easiest to assume that something is incredibly complex. We all like to believe that there's a clever, sociological explanation for the terrifyingly indiscriminate violence of hooligans and terrorists. And perhaps you have a Facebook friend who buys into elaborate conspiracy theories to explain all the unpleasantness she worries about. This way of thinking may cause us fewer headaches than the idea that life is chaotic and horrible things happen.

Business consultants and spiritual coaches have made a career out of this housefly. Nobody wants to hear that the problem they've been struggling with for years doesn't

> really amount to much. That's not to say that we use our brain capacity to really get to the bottom of complex explanations. We just *feel* as though we understand. This is known as the **illusion of explanatory depth**: because you use them every day, you may think you know how your laptop, car or bike works. But could you actually draw a brake mechanism?

We love choice, but hate choosing

Tokyo is abuzz with exotic houseflies. The countless illuminations in Akihabara, the thousands of signposts at Shinjuku Station, they all seem to be sending you in different directions. Yet one of the most fascinating housefly effects in this metropolis reflects the other side of Japan: minimalism. The fancy neighbourhood of Ginza is home to Morioka Shoten, a bookshop. Literally, a shop selling a book. In his now world-famous business, Yoshiyuki Morioka offers one carefully curated title every week. And it's a great success. Understandably. People like choice, but they hate having to choose. Not only does it take up another chunk of that limited brain capacity, but you may also regret it later. Give people too many options and they'd rather not pick anything at all. Alternatively, help them choose and reap the rewards.

A classic experiment carried out by researchers at the universities of Stanford and Columbia illustrates the housefly effect of excessive or limited choice.[7] They set up a stall with jam in a large supermarket, offering a selection of twenty-four flavours on one occasion and only six on another. The second stand sold many more jars, with 12 percent of passers-by purchasing something compared to 2 percent of those who had a plethora of choice.

Why? When faced with twenty-four options, people are more likely to disengage due to choice overload, a much-documented phenomenon that we're all familiar with. The panicky feeling that comes over you in a huge department store has a name: FOBO, Fear of Better Options.* What if there's something better out there? One shop that embodies this principle can be found – where else – in Los Angeles. Record collectors from all over the world flock to Amoeba Music's vast selection, only to admit later on that it wasn't the paradise they'd envisioned. This was Tim's experience: with a few deep breaths and a nifty little list you'll come out the other end. But so much choice – it's not exactly fun.

With its micro assortment, Morioka Shoten undoubtedly has much happier shoppers. But why is that? One theory is that your brain likes to avoid regret. The Tokyo bookshop minimises the risk of buyer's remorse. You can't buy too much, miss anything or afterwards think 'damn, I should have asked about that other title'. Amoeba Music, on the other hand, is a minefield of regret. You bet your bottom dollar that on your return home you'll suddenly think of other items you should have looked for. And that the one record you thought was too expensive turns out to be even pricier in your home country. And the message from your subconscious? This is taking up too much energy, let's get a move on! That said, more choice doesn't always lead to more stress. A meta-analysis of numerous variations on the jam experiment reveals that choice overload is particularly acute when people have no strong preferences, when they are unfamiliar with the options available or when those alternatives are very similar and difficult to compare.[8]

---

* Coined by Patrick McGinnis, the same man who came up with FOMO (Fear Of Missing Out), about which more elsewhere in this book.

Would you rather?

The trend for retailers with a purposely limited assortment is also making inroads in the Netherlands. Czaar Peterstraat in Amsterdam is home to a peanut-butter shop, an olive-oil store, a whisky seller, a cheesemonger and a purveyor of coffee beans.* Likewise, a growing number of new fashion labels now sell just a single item: a long T-shirt, a pair of functional cargo pants, comfortable high heels. Even so, large stores with an extensive range of products still attract far more customers. The most successful among them take a clever approach to the dilemma of choice versus choosing. They draw you in with the promise of a broad selection and deploy all kinds of houseflies to make it easier for you to part with your cash. This starts with subdividing the place into sections, aisles and shelves and introducing an intuitive hierarchy to them ('regular' in the middle, expensive just above and cheap close to floor level). And then there are the lists with tips, the menus of the week, beers of the month, special offers of the day – all clever shortcuts to avoid choice overload.

You can apply the same principle in your own life by making small changes to the way you present choices, a process called choice architecture. Here's what happens when you give people two options. Ask your friends 'where shall we go for dinner?' and you'll still be wandering round town hours later, tired and famished. But ask 'burgers or sushi?' and it won't take them long to reach a decision. In rhetoric this is known as *the fallacy of the false dilemma*, but behavioural scientists have come up with a less forbidding term: choice reduction. It's another one of those techniques that are frequently harnessed by populists. In the runup to the 2020 elections, Trump presented voters with a list of 'choices', which effectively boiled down to 'Do you want Trump, or do you

---

* The street was named the Netherlands' most charming shopping district, but 'least efficient supermarket' is another way of looking at it.

want your house to be torched by rabid hordes of radical Communists?' Well, if you put it that way... It's like the game 'would you rather?' An American chain of clothing stores draws on this in their changing rooms with hooks saying ABSOLUTELY and POSSIBLY... Customers who've tried something on are forced to hang the garments on one of the two. And when you've left something on ABSOLUTELY there's every chance that you end up buying it.* Here's another example: on entering, an Asian retailer offers a choice of colour-coded baskets. Blue means I'd like assistance; red, I'd like to shop on my own. Customers choose the one that reflects their needs – and forget about the third option: no basket. And there you have it, mission accomplished, as shoppers tend to buy more with a basket in their hands.†

The decoy as secret weapon

But what if you give people two options and they choose the wrong one? This is what happened to *The Economist*. The magazine was keen for people to choose the expensive subscription covering both print and web access but found that two-thirds of subscribers opted for the cheap online-only version. The marketing department decided to experiment and included a lousy third option: a **decoy**. Print-only, for the same high price as print and web combined, this was essentially the expensive option's 'ugly sibling'. Needless to say, nobody fell for it. But now, suddenly, a majority went for the expensive alternative.

---

* The retailer was clever enough not to add a hook saying *NO WAY!*
† You'll be relieved to hear that there was no ulterior motive behind the compulsory use of shopping trolleys in Dutch supermarkets during the coronavirus pandemic.

> This ugly sibling is a shrewd housefly. As your focus inadvertently shifts to two of the three offers, you take another look at them. 'Is it me, or does that third option make no sense whatsoever? Who'd choose that one? Surely the other one's *far* better?' And before you know it, you've clicked on the best of the expensive subscriptions without giving the cheaper one a second thought.

Let's return to those friends of yours. There you are, cleverly asking 'burgers or sushi?' because you fancy a spicy tuna roll yourself. But the group is leaning towards the former. In that case, you could say: 'burgers, ready-made sushi to-go or that authentic sushi joint where, for the same price, it's prepared right in front of you?' Another tactic is to get people to answer a totally different question, also known as choice substitution. Someone in the UK designed a clever ashtray that asked, 'Who is the best player in the world?' People voted by dropping their cigarette butt into a bin with the name Ronaldo on it or into one labelled Messi. Of course, the underlying question was: are you going to drop your fag end on the ground or will you dispose of it responsibly? Because it wasn't made explicit, many more people chose the desirable option.

No further action is needed: the power of the standard option

Before we go any further, here's a formality from our publisher's legal department: by continuing, you agree to the privacy policy and general terms and conditions that can be found on https://bromvliegeffect.nl/voorwaarden. Please use Google translate if you don't read Dutch.

We'll wait. It may take a while.

So, what did you make of them?

If you're anything like the rest of humankind, you didn't read them and blindly consented (or else you wouldn't be reading this, right?). That's exactly what happens on websites. But why is that? Because it's presented as the standard option, as something perfectly normal that just happens when you don't do anything. And we accentuated that with the words 'formality' and 'general'. You were given a choice, but reading on didn't really feel like a conscious decision; it was just business as usual. And your brain was pretty happy about that.

If there's one thing the brain likes even better than an easy choice, it's no choice at all. Not making choices equals no stress, no regret and, when everything goes wrong, no responsibility. And besides, if we're honest, we often don't really know what we want anyway. Each option has pros and cons and weighing them up can be hard. Presenting something as the best of both worlds is a tried-and-tested concept in advertising: tackles both dry and chesty coughs! Why choose between long *and* full eyelashes? An even more effective way of saving people the trouble of having to choose is by earmarking one option as the **default**. The default is what you get when you don't make a choice. It can be seen in emails from businesses saying *if you agree to the terms, no further action is needed,* and in subscriptions that are automatically renewed. Such a standard option produces a very potent housefly effect.

Social factors can come into this, with people assuming that something has become the standard option because it's popular and therefore unlikely to be a disastrous choice. But there's more to it than that. Let's start with the best-known example: organ donation. For many years, Tim worked on campaigns aimed at encouraging the Dutch to sign up to the donor register, for instance with appeals to self-determination ('my body, my choice'). These campaigns were relatively successful. At 27.5 percent, the Netherlands had a higher percentage of registered organ donors than countries such as Germany (12 percent) and Denmark (4.25 percent).[9] A fine achievement, until you saw the figures for, say, Belgium (98 percent) and Austria (99.98 percent). The difference lay in the opt-out system used in these countries. The Dutch, Germans and Danes had to give their active consent to be a donor, Austrians and Belgians had to withdraw it.* Unsurprisingly, the Netherlands has now also made donation the standard option. No advertising campaign can compete with this.

It's important to recognise that a standard option can have a huge impact, especially on major (and therefore difficult) decisions, not least because you can't avoid designating one option as the default.† So which one do you pick? An informed choice can do a lot of good. For instance, employees in the United States aren't automatically enrolled in their company's pension scheme when they're hired but, as soon as it's offered as the standard option, there's a significant increase in uptake. Whenever Eva or Tim touch on this topic at presentations, there'll be some audience members who say: 'I can see through these standard options and that actually puts me off.' Fair enough, some defaults are downright despicable. Here too Donald J. Trump takes the biscuit. A deviously hidden ticked box meant that his donors paid double what they thought was a one-off donation – *weekly*. That's

---

* Though it's worth noting that when you look at the percentage of organs that are actually donated, the differences are far less pronounced. In countries where donation is the norm, there will be other opportunities for opting out, for instance when the next-of-kin choose not to donate.

† You could of course have a ballot that allocates a random 50 percent of the population to the donor register and leaves out the other half. People are then free to swap. But given the huge housefly effect of defaults, that might boil down to leaving their decision to chance.

counterproductive. Research has shown that transparency about a default can actually make it more effective. If the standard option is in people's interest and you're quite open about that, most will be fine with it.[10]

> ### A painful asterisk
>
> One example hits very close to home. Eva once went to a party to celebrate a friend paying off her student loan. It was a huge occasion, because the woman was forty by the time she finally settled the debt. The root of the problem was probably a tiny asterisk. The application form that the friend (and Eva herself) had filled in twenty years ago had asked:
>
> How much would you like to borrow?
>
> [*] maximum amount
>
> [ ] other, please specify: ...
>
> What would you do? That's right, 68 percent of prospective students borrowed as much as they could. Shortly after Eva and her friend had been railroaded by this housefly, a webmaster at DUO, the student finance company, removed the asterisk. Small tweak, small difference? No, from that moment onwards, the percentage of new students borrowing the maximum amount halved.[11]

Alongside the defaults used by businesses and public bodies, your brain provides its own 'standard options'. Quick, name the most important scientist of all time! So who were you thinking of? Albert Einstein? Many people do. The question is why. Perhaps you have

The power of convenience

a physics degree and think that despite the merits of Feynman, Oppenheimer and Curie, Einstein remains the greatest. But chances are you're less of a fan and more into Kahneman, yet still thought of Einstein first. This is the housefly of mental availability. Something pops into your head unprompted, so your mind subconsciously has it down as significant, representative and widespread.

This can be handy, but in many cases this mental availability simply stems from how often and how recently you've encountered something, say in the media. It explains why we overestimate the chances of a plane crash or the impact of a new technology. These tend to receive extensive news coverage, unlike the far greater number of car accidents and existing solutions that work perfectly well. It's known as **availability bias**. 'Mental availability' is the holy grail of advertising. You may be gasping at the lame jokes and the overblown promises and think, 'I'm not falling for that', but the question isn't whether or not you're swayed by ads. No, the question is what brand will 'spontaneously' spring to mind the next time you need razor blades, coffee or shampoo. It turns out that those with higher mental availability are picked more readily, which means their market share will increase faster. And that availability has little to do with substantial differences. Healthier ingredients, better quality – these are all very well, but mental availability rests primarily on the exposure a brand receives, and whether it has something distinctive that makes it memorable. Golden arches, an annoying jingle, a *ding dong pizza* slogan... it all helps catapult a brand to the forefront of your mind, so your brain doesn't have to make any tough decisions and can just switch to its default. To quote a classic line from market research: 'Advertising has no effect on me; I only buy the big brands.'

The power of habit

As we've seen, brains don't like to choose. So when yours has finally, after much agonising, come to a decision, it doesn't like to see it challenged. And because people like convenience, a choice often turns into a habit. Nothing is as easy as doing what you've always done. If you stick to existing practices, your grey cells can just phone it in and won't have to make any decisions at all. Hitting snooze once, eating breakfast, brushing your teeth, showering, getting dressed, grabbing your bag, hopping on your bike... it's all done on autopilot, leaving your brain free to get angry with the news or listen to a fun podcast on behavioural science. The most extreme form of routine behaviour is sleepwalking, during which people can go through something like an entire morning ritual without waking up. A clever evolutionary feat, you might think. Yet habits get a bad rap. They're an expedient target for stand-up comedians (who, night after night, tell the same jokes about other people's humdrum lives), and ideal if you're keen to score likes with inspirational quotes on LinkedIn. 'Break out of your comfort zone!'* But when Tim worked on a campaign with the slogan 'escape the grind' he quickly learned that consumers aren't interested. What may look like being stuck in a rut to others is an enjoyable routine to us. It explains the well-known marketing fact that families have a repertoire of around nine recipes. Anyone trying to expand it will probably find that they've bitten off more than they can chew.

The coronavirus pandemic gave us daily reminders of just how set in our ways we are. You could tell from the moaning on social media ('I always celebrate my birthday with the neighbours and now that's not allowed. The government should go!') and from some wonderfully absurd trends in the travel industry, with huge

---

* The person posting this usually means: my colleagues, boss and clients should move into *my* comfort zone.

numbers of people booking flights to... nowhere. While lockdown rules meant they wouldn't be allowed through immigration in another country, they could still travel there. So that's what they did, only to head straight back on arrival, without ever leaving the airport or railway station. It gave them that familiar taste of travel, and that was enough. Airlines capitalised on this with special offers for 'scenic flights'. The one over Australia offered by Qantas sold out in less than ten minutes. If that wasn't bizarre enough, Singapore Airlines launched a plane dining experience – on the runway. Yes, that's right, the discomfort of eating in a cramped seat without travelling anywhere. Again, there was plenty of demand. But surely we're talking about a luxury experience in business class? While some did indeed pay hundreds of dollars for the privilege, most of the diners ate at a rickety little tray table in economy class. It's a whole new take on the motto, 'It's about the journey, not the destination.' The airlines made very clever use of the habitual housefly.

They're not the only ones. Businesses exploit our habits in all kinds of ways. The clever ones do so by *not* breaking our routines if at all possible. Tim once discovered that one of his clients had notched up a huge increase in sales. He'd already cleared space on his mantelpiece for the shiny advertising award when he realised that this growth wasn't down to his brilliant campaign. The rival brand had overhauled its packaging, meaning that consumers could no longer shop on autopilot and therefore switched in their droves. Ouch. This happened to orange juice brand Tropicana, which in 2009 spent 35 million dollars on the launch of its new branding and subsequently saw revenue drop by 20 percent. It makes you think about marketing terms such as brand loyalty and (bullshit bingo cards at the ready) *brand love*. Are people really enamoured with 'their' brand of frozen meatballs? Or are they loyal to their own choices and habits? The latter seems more likely. We like to be consistent in our decision making, as it conserves energy. And from an evolutionary standpoint, it's good to not be seen as fickle or hypocritical, qualities that aren't conducive to group survival. We still slam politicians for 'U-turning', as if arriving at new insights is scandalous somehow. Behaviour change campaigns often rely on such appeals to consistency: 'You wouldn't steal a television... downloading pirated films is stealing.'

If the desirable behaviour is already firmly entrenched, organisations do well to let sleeping dogs lie. Name changes, emails to keep your customers engaged – it can all be counterproductive. So what if people aren't yet habitually doing what you'd like them to? For that you have a bug hotel full of houseflies at your disposal. It won't come as a surprise to you that they swarm around our heads all day long. A fairly innocuous example is the coffee shop loyalty card. By the time you've reached that '12th Frappuccino free!', you're well on your way to developing a habit. That's why they're generous with the extra stamps, especially at the start of a new loyalty card.* It's a principle known as **endowed progress**: when you're halfway through, you feel as though you've earned something, and it would be a shame to squander that. Your brain doesn't like to see you waste energy, money and effort. The same principle is built into apps in the guise of *streaks*. You've posted videos six days in a row now, so create more content today and don't risk breaking the streak and losing out on a fine achievement or badge! It's a feature of online shopping too. Once you've made it to step five of the checkout process, it would be a shame to drop out.

The tradition of celebrating wedding and work anniversaries could well be rooted in the same psychology: achievements *avant la lettre* helping people to continue what they've started. It becomes just that little bit more manipulative when companies

---

* Sorry to break it to you, but the barista isn't flirting.

The power of convenience

organise their customers into levels. 'As a gold member you have access to special privileges. Order X amount now to claim your reward!' Until recently, this 'use it or lose it' kind of tactic was also deployed in more contentious areas, such as the sale of alcohol.

But the most addictive manifestations of this housefly can be found on your phone. Or did you think that checking it, on average, about a hundred times a day is something you do entirely of your own free will? Behind every app you just can't close are specially reared killer houseflies that create not only habits but outright addictions. Thanks to habit guru Nir Eyal,[12] whose Hook Model taught armies of app developers exactly how to get users hooked, nothing is left to chance.

1. Give users a trigger, such as a notification sound or a red number next to the app icon. The brain interprets them as an unfinished task that it wants to complete (a common housefly known as the **Zeigarnik effect**).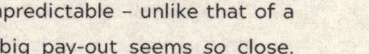

2. This is then followed by a user action, by you opening the app or checking your mail.

3. And here's the crucial thing: it's the **variable reward** that makes the app addictive. A notification has popped up! An exciting message from your crush? No, it just says, 'People you may know'. Annoying, but the addiction lies in all those moments when you miss the boat. People will insert coins into a slot machine for hours on end because the reward is variable and unpredictable – unlike that of a coffee dispenser. And because the big pay-out seems *so* close. The wheels on a fruit machine, the pictures on a scratch card: often you're just a cherry or a dollar bill away. It's the anticipation that gives you the (dopamine) kick that you want to experience over and over again.

The Housefly Effect

4. The final component of Eyal's devious fish hook consists of investments (or sunk costs), of putting time and effort into the app. You work on your profile, like your friends' photos, join a group, post a picture... those investments increase the likelihood that you'll return soon. And after a while it's unthinkable that you'll ever uninstall the app and risk losing your likes, photos and friends and wasting all that effort. As an app junkie you may not be sleeping under a bridge, but you do sleep with your phone within easy reach.

There's good news too. Once you know this, you can actually train and harness the habitual housefly to finally develop the good habits you've been dreaming of: reading more books, exercising more often, getting up earlier, all good intentions that frequently flounder. There's a yawning gulf between what you want to do and what you actually do. The scientific term for this is **intention–action gap**. Perhaps you've set the bar very high for yourself, so your goals are only attainable when you're supermotivated. Two hours of exercise a day? You betcha! But let's face it, motivation and priorities fluctuate. If your enthusiasm is flagging when you haven't cemented a habit yet, you're bound to fail and feel more demotivated than ever. Now's the time to make Silicon Valley's crafty techniques work for *you*. Keep track of your 'streak', preferably in a visible place like a fun, retro chalkboard: X number of consecutive days without sweets. When you meet your target, why not give yourself a reward (a pair of shoes, a nice coffee, something that makes you happy or you can show off to others)? Set alarms to remind yourself. Or let your new routine piggyback on an existing one. American habit expert BJ Fogg recommends doing a push-up every time you've used the toilet, for example. Then there's the brilliant Australian campaign that encourages people to replace the battery in their smoke detector when they change the clocks back at the end of daylight saving. It's an easy association to make since you're on a ladder anyway, adjusting the time.

The power of convenience

In short, this housefly is a creature of habit, albeit one that can learn new tricks. Take advantage of it!

A fly in the ointment

We've seen that our brain likes to take the path of least resistance, that this is in fact a physical necessity. It follows that, subconsciously, we like to avoid difficult decisions – by doing nothing, by sticking to habits, by choosing what feels like the easiest option. Does that mean that it's *always* best to make things as easy as possible, to not let people think too much and instead try to create a standard option or a mindless routine? That's not the note on which we want to conclude this chapter. When in doubt, keep it simple. This usually holds true. Then again, a little bit of effort can produce a housefly effect too. A good example is a stand-up comedian telling a joke in such a way that you arrive at the gag line at exactly the right time. This is called the **generation effect**. Because your brain generated the punchline, that joke will stay with you.

Advertising legend George Lois drew on this principle when he created Tommy Hilfiger's first campaign. A giant billboard on Times Square read: 'THE 4 GREAT AMERICAN DESIGNERS FOR MEN ARE', followed by initials and dashes. A fun game of hangman for passers-by, who quickly worked out that R____ L_____ stood for Ralph Lauren and also recognised C(alvin) K(lein) and P(erry) E(llis). But who was this T____ H_____? Lois had an excellent feel for what's known as the *Information Gap Theory*. Your brain becomes curious when it stumbles upon a gap in your knowledge and wants to fill it. But bear in mind that people aren't curious about things they know absolutely nothing about. Nor is their interest piqued when they think (rightly or because they overestimate their own knowledge) they already know virtually everything there is to know about a topic. The midpoint between these two is where we find the *Curiosity Zone*: when you know that you know quite a bit, but not everything. Clickbait operates on the principle of exploiting this gap. *Are you familiar with these twelve housefly effects? Number eight will astonish you!*

Still, we advise caution when it comes to that little bit of effort. A study once suggested that a harder-to-read typeface would help people better remember the substance of a text.[13] It prompted a team of scientists to develop a font that would provide the ideal ratio between effort and comprehension. Great idea, and had it been effective we'd have used it in our book. But sadly, there's no proof that it works. The perceived effect may have been down to the fact that a distinctive typeface stands out and commands our attention (see the **Von Restorff effect** in chapter 6). There's far more evidence that extra effort is off-putting. Other researchers corroborated this by describing a simple physical exercise and asking people how long they reckoned it might take them. One group received the instructions in a clear sans serif, the other in an elegant, but less readable font. Both were asked to estimate the time spent doing six to ten repetitions. The responses were markedly different. Those who'd been given the 'easy' typeface thought it would take them around eight minutes, compared to fifteen for the group with the elegant font.[14] And anyone with a passing acquaintance with the lazy housefly will know by now that the chances of this group actually doing them are minimal.

We've encountered quite a few houseflies and concepts in this chapter. But what's the main takeaway for you, aside from being able to casually drop nudging and sludging into a conversation? The key thing to remember is this: if you want people to do something, don't make it harder than necessary, and preferably make it easy, obvious and fun. Check what obstacles you could remove before resorting to persuasive tactics and information, and don't make things appear more complex than they are. Communicate in plain language. Split tasks into chunks and draw up a phased plan. Avoid choice overload: don't give people too many options and, where possible, simplify the process. Think long and hard about the default, about what happens when somebody doesn't make a choice. Switch off those notifications.

And finally, remember: 'simple is always better' is a little too simplistic.

> The pain fly beats a hasty retreat at the slightest threat.

Musca doloris

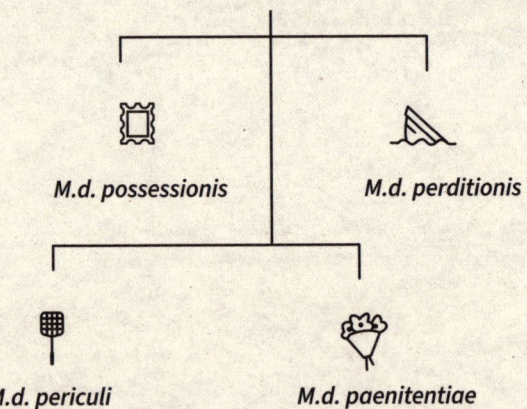

M.d. possessionis

M.d. perditionis

M.d. periculi

M.d. paenitentiae

Chapter 3

Pain and how to turn it into gain

Musca doloris or 'pain fly'

Subspecies: *M.d. possessionis* (possession), *M.d. perditionis* (loss aversion), *M.d. periculi* (risk avoidance), *M.d. paenitentiae* (anticipated regret)

Jittery fly that beats a hasty retreat when confronted with potential threat. Often perceives danger where there is none. Likes to collect possessions of all kinds and defends them with its life. Persistently present where financial decisions are made, but also often found in holiday parks and other relatively safe places. Marketers make liberal use of this fly. Feel free to use this book as a fly swatter, as *Musca doloris* is far from a threatened species.

In October 1997 Tim went to withdraw cash from an ATM. He'd received good news: an offer of his first job as a real advertising copywriter. He entered his card and PIN, selected the amount and walked home, head in the clouds, only to realise that he'd left his fifty-euro note in the cash machine. Back he went, but the person after him had pocketed the cash. What's so surprising about this story? The fact that Tim can still recall it. No doubt during this period he also sometimes received book or record vouchers (his favourite gift) for around the same value. But he's forgotten those. That loss from long ago, however, is etched into his memory, and in this respect he's far from unique. Losing something hits us all much harder than receiving the same item. Think how angry you are when someone pinches your rusty bike. In fact it makes such an impression that our brains will do anything to avoid such an unpleasant experi‑

ence. The consequences of **loss aversion**, that tendency to avoid pain, can be seen everywhere, from the company failing to draw a line under a hopeless prestige project to the young child in tears about juice spilt over an old drawing (when they don't so much as glance at other doodles at the back of a drawer). It can be seen in all our daily lives too, because what we have, we'd like to hold onto, and this results in the strangest of housefly effects.

All our earthly possessions

Eva's father has five garages. Dining-room chairs, rocking horses and cans of paint keep company with components of two Citroën 2CVs and guitar-shaped radios. The only thing these items have in common is that they once passed through his hands and for that reason alone he's reluctant to get rid of them. There's nothing wrong with them and they're sure to come in handy some time. For the moment he's even hanging onto his (unread) copy of Marie Kondo's book, advocating a strict method of extreme decluttering. Do you recognise this behaviour? Eva was very much reassured during her degree when she learned that this tendency to collect things is in part inherited but that *everyone* is to some extent afflicted by it. It's such a widespread human phenomenon that there's a term for it. You're probably thinking of 'hoarding', but we mean the everyday variant: the **endowment effect**, first described by Richard Thaler and robustly researched thereafter.[1] In a study Thaler gave university mugs to half of the student participants and bars of chocolate to the other half. They were then permitted to come to him and exchange their gift. You'd think that both groups had the same number of chocolate lovers, but those with a mug didn't want to swap, and nor did those with chocolate. A follow-up experiment showed how much more people value something once it's in their possession. Those who didn't have a mug were prepared to pay on average 2.25 dollars for one, but students who'd been given one suddenly felt that those mugs were worth more than double and demanded 5.25 dollars for them.

Students aren't the only ones to suffer from this endowment effect. (Eva's father would be sure to put the mug in the garage too.) Even chimpanzees become attached to their possessions. In a study the great apes got to choose between an ice lolly and a lick of peanut butter. Sixty percent of the apes opted for peanut butter, but that changed when they were given peanut butter first and permitted to exchange it for an ice lolly. Then as many as 80 percent chose peanut butter. Clearly some of these primates preferred peanut butter purely because they already had it.

This housefly effect also applies in the real world of buying and selling. Think of sites like eBay and Gumtree: sellers often set the price too high from an objective point of view, because owners mistakenly see their worn-out trainers as perfectly wearable. Shareholders often hold onto their shares for too long, because they think the price will rally – it's *their* share after all. The endowment effect therefore blocks the market. But these two examples may of course also be perfectly sensible: perhaps it's smart to keep hold of your property and even to overestimate it (just as you overestimate yourself). That way you negotiate harder and all the more convincingly.

Doctor, I'm suffering from payment pain

Of course the endowment effect also clings to money. It hurts to pay. According to a much-discussed study,[2] your brain really does perceive something like 'pain in the purse'. The researchers examined brain activity in people who were asked to consider a purchase. They could see a response in the brain to weighing up the gain and the pain of the purchase, revealing that pain can be taken pretty literally in this context. When the researchers showed an excessive price label for an attractive product, activity increased in the insula, the part of the brain presumed to play a key role in processing pain. In short, whether you graze your knee or see a high price, the reaction is the same: ouch!

There are also houseflies that ensure that you feel that pain less sharply. That's great for the person wanting to sell you something. The most painful way to pay is probably in cash, especially after the pleasure of the purchase has passed. Which, in fact, is precisely what happens in a restaurant. Comedian Jerry Seinfeld has a wonderful sketch about this, in which he recounts how people who have just stuffed themselves with food, trousers unbuttoned, look indignantly at the bill and say, 'We're not hungry now, why are we buying all this food?' The pain tends to be softened with an after-dinner mint for the road and a cheerful goodbye from the waiter – none of which are coincidental, of course.

Even more effective are the plastic coins at festivals. Festival currencies don't feel like money, so you spend them much more easily. In fact this was first invented in casinos, although they're called chips there, and of course they're rather easier than coins to shove onto red in one big pile. But even normal money can be made less painful with simple houseflies. For instance, contactless payment hurts less than the old-fashioned way of settling the bill by cash or typing in your PIN. And sellers like to talk about so many 'K' or 'big ones' or even leave out euphemisms for thousands altogether and say you can have that car for twenty-eight.* In restaurants there are often no currency signs on the menu. Sometimes they even leave off points, commas or other symbols that invoke the association with price. The savviest chefs even write out the price in words: 'bread with olive oil – fifteen'. You don't feel a thing!

What if you've really spent too much and you're deep in the red? In common parlance, dissatisfied people reach for 'comfort food', and indeed, it's been demonstrated that financial dissatisfaction drives people to eat.[3†] The researchers cultivated 'monetarily dissatisfied' people and 'monetarily satisfied' people by asking them about their bank account balances. One group were asked to answer on a scale from 1 to 9, running from '0 to 50 dollars' through to 'more than 400 dollars'. For the other group the scale varied

---

* But only for a trendy type like you. Then they'll go and fight those imaginary bosses in the back office, of course, who'll cry when they see this discount! We could fill another couple of books with the car or kitchen dealer houseflies.
† Demonstrated, in fact, in a laboratory – but it was only a single study, so until further notice take these results with a pinch of salt.

between '0 to 500 dollars' and 'more than 400,000 dollars'. If you answer this question yourself, you'll probably notice that the second question brings you to the lower end of the scale, giving you the sense of having relatively little money. Having been manipulated in this way, the participants were allowed to choose between two dishes, for instance strawberries with cream and strawberries with chocolate mousse. An online panel had assessed these products as being equally tasty and equally expensive; the only difference was how energy-rich the panel believed them to be. The 'dissatisfied' participants systematically picked more calorific foods than the satisfied participants (in the above example, the cream).

In a subsequent experiment new participants were asked to estimate the nutritional value of a plate of brownies. Some knew that they would then be permitted to eat a brownie. Once again, half were first made to feel satisfied with their bank balance and half dissatisfied. Satisfied people were reasonably successful in estimating the nutritional value, independent of whether they were permitted to eat a brownie. Dissatisfied people, on the other hand, underestimated the calorie content of the brownies if they were permitted to eat one, and overestimated it if they were not expecting to eat them. The dissatisfied participants ended up eating more of the brownies than the satisfied subjects.

When you feel poor, you exhibit less healthy behaviour, so don't go thinking being fat is a choice. The relationship between your finances and your health is complex and is only partially steered by houseflies. But to be on the safe side, it might be best not to spend your lunch break surfing Rightmove, gawping at expensive mansions.

The slightest chance of a major disaster

'You only want the very best quality.' You can just hear the smooth advertising voice. And perhaps you think: too right, so I'll buy a well-known brand of toaster. But what do you really think is more important: that a toaster still produces perfect toast after fifteen years, or that you can be sure it's not going to electrocute you tomorrow? Probably the latter. This is known as the **certainty effect**. We'll go out of our way to avoid the slightest chance of disaster: **risk avoidance**. Even top footballers go to more trouble to avoid risk than to win. After all, it's well known that penalties aimed higher in the goal are stopped considerably less frequently than 'low' penalties, yet all those handsomely paid top footballers shoot low far more often than high. There's a simple reason for that: if you shoot too high, you miss the goal altogether, which has the same consequences for the match as if the ball had been blocked. But the fallout is far worse: 'Flipping heck, he's overshot!' So it's best to try and avoid that increased risk with a low kick.[4]

The low penalty is just one example of an important principle: if you're trying to motivate people, don't (only) tell them why your suggestion is the best. Make them also feel that it's low-risk, or that the risk of not doing it is very high. Sometimes a little bit of certainty can conceal a big housefly effect!

Many companies with a strong, well-known brand continue to benefit from this type of tactic. People aren't so much paying extra because they think the product is better as because they think there's a smaller chance they'll end up with junk. After all, a big name like that has something to lose and will pay attention to quality. Even if a well-known brand actually does disappoint, at least no one's going to ridicule you for your choice. A drill from a well-known brand can just as easily break, but it won't earn you a rollicking from your brother-in-law: 'You get what you pay for!' The brand functions as a kind of incantation against regret. One of the founders of McDonald's wisely said that people don't want the best hamburger; they just want the same as last time. Guaranteed More or Less Okay*: it doesn't work as a slogan on a poster, but secretly that's the reason why safe, predictable holiday parks are always full, as are flights to destinations with guaranteed sun or snow.

Admittedly, planes are also full of people who do wish to try West African street food or go rafting down the Amazon. Clearly, we don't all avoid risk to the same extent. Waiters can spot them a mile away: the regulars who like to be on the safe side and keep on ordering the same dish, even if they might discover something tastier if they took a gamble once in a while. Others seek out extreme risks, climbing K2 or investing in start-ups. Such personality differences in risk tolerance are not only human, they're deeply rooted in our brains. Birds too (great tits and starlings to be precise)[5] can be categorised according to a similar neuronal system into risk seekers and risk avoiders, with the latter staying a long time, possibly too long, in a familiar feeding ground.

You might expect that natural selection would do away with individuals who are systematically wrong in their assessment of risk. Nevertheless, that distribution of personalities persists. A group of American biologists and computer scientists offered an explanation and tested it with the help of a simulation.[6] The researchers programmed a model environment in which, like God during Creation, they distributed different risk personalities among their simulated individuals. All made one important decision in their lives: their choice of partner. Some were satisfied with an option that was 'good enough', no more, no less – someone with little positive or negative influence on their chances of survival. Others preferred to look for the perfect match, with the risk of ending up with a really bad mate. In the simulation those personalities were inherited, as in birds and humans. That meant that the individuals with the best partners on average had the most offspring, who in turn were roughly as choosy (risk-seeking) or easily satisfied (risk-averse).

The result was that in groups of fewer than 150 individuals, approximately the size of group our ancestors on the savannah lived in, it turned out to be advantageous to avoid risks. At least, in such important, once-in-a-lifetime decisions. The one-off nature of the choices was a determining factor. If decisions weren't repeated often, as in the choice of a partner, more risk avoiders survived. For decisions repeated on a daily basis, such as the choice of feeding ground, more risk seekers in the population survived. The researchers concluded that one-off decisions were probably crucial to the way our brains deal with risk.

We use those same brains to weigh up both menu choices and potential partners. The average person is a little too cautious with menu choices but, even after thousands of generations in the simulation, a few daredevils remained, both in starlings and in humans. So practical advice for choice of partner for single people would be: stop searching for the one and instead, in risk-averse fashion, pick a mate who's good enough. Save risk-taking for the menu at your regular restaurant.

On average, people don't like risks. You don't need a scientific experiment to tell you that; it's evident in daily life. We buy toaster insurance and pay the excess on hire cars, we remain in boring jobs and familiar restaurants; all due to our extreme risk aversion. After all, our brains evolved to avoid danger, and certainly not to intentionally seek it out. You see that in a housefly, known as **omission bias**. A risk that is naturally present when we do nothing (omission here referring to inaction) is easier for us to accept than one we sought out or created ourselves. Tim bought his skateboarding daughter a helmet, knowing that falling is naturally part and parcel of skateboarding, but he became a nervous wreck when he heard that a helmet worn wrongly increases the chance of neck injury, because he himself was responsible for this particular risk. Of course, this also weighs heavily in medical decisions. The risk of a rare side effect or complication of a medicine, vaccine or intervention can be small, but it may well *feel* more intense than the risk a patient runs due to their illness.

> **Risk avoidance for a relaxed ride**
>
> Most people don't make a habit of parking their car up a tree, so why would you pay the car rental company 78 pounds extra to avoid a minimal chance of having to pay 1,000 pounds insurance excess? The rental company properly rubs your nose in it: you'd have to pay the first 1,000 pounds if the car were stolen, you were involved in a collision or you lost your car keys. Yes, one of those things has happened to most of us at some point, so it feels realistic, and 78 pounds is clearly less than 1,000 pounds, so it's an easy calculation to make.
>
> The nice thing is, the chance of your driving into something is reduced too, because you're less stressed about your parallel parking when you've paid off the risk.

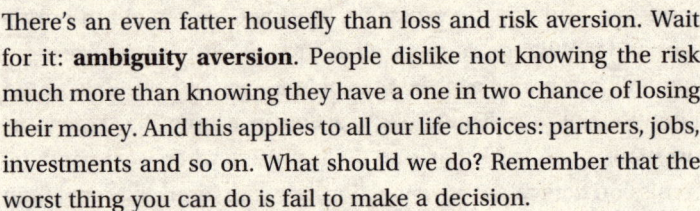

There's an even fatter housefly than loss and risk aversion. Wait for it: **ambiguity aversion**. People dislike not knowing the risk much more than knowing they have a one in two chance of losing their money. And this applies to all our life choices: partners, jobs, investments and so on. What should we do? Remember that the worst thing you can do is fail to make a decision.

Closing the door

We now know that loss is painful and that taking risks hurts, but why? Because your self-flagellation for making the wrong choice hits you the hardest. Actively saying no hurts, whether it's to a holiday home, a potential partner or a boring project: it's unpalatable to have to close the door on something. The **anticipated regret** plays a big role in decisions. It's awkward, because we're not good at predicting how we'll feel in a particular event. If you ask people to predict how happy they would be if they won the lottery, they overestimate their happiness enormously; after six months there's no difference in perceived happiness between lottery winners and losers.[7] Generally such prizes lead to all kinds of unexpected misery; from divorces and begging letters from friends to resentful looks from the neighbours who never bought a ticket.[8]* At the other end of the spectrum, we also overestimate the extent to which our lives would be turned upside down if something bad were to happen. After a leg amputation people tend to be back at their previous level of happiness quite quickly. So remember: you'll generally experience less regret than you think; failing to make a decision is worse than making the wrong decision.†

Why do people avoid decisions, sometimes even so long that they shoot themselves in the foot? Behavioural scientist Dan Ariely set up an experiment to investigate what people find difficult about psychologically closing doors.[9] He developed a game for this. Imagine you're given twelve clicks of the mouse and can win money by clicking on one of three doors with slot machines behind each. But watch out, every time you change door, it costs you a click. You begin by testing it out. Behind the left-hand door you win 1 cent, 5 cents, 11 cents and 3 cents in your first few goes. You then look behind the middle door, where you win 4 cents, 2 cents, 1 cent, 1 cent, 3 cents. The right-hand door gives you 7, 10, 2, 18, 5, 8, and so on, eventually tending towards an average of 7 cents

---

* No, we're not speaking from personal experience – economists don't gamble, and Tim prefers to go to Las Vegas.
† Tim has adopted the term *perfectionihilism* for this: doing nothing because anything you might do has to seem perfect in advance. The 'if-we're-going-to-do-it-we're-going-to-do-it-right' effect? Paradoxically enough, that's precisely what brings regret.

per click. Of course most participants soon realised that the right-hand door on average gave them the most, and after a couple of switches the majority of players stayed there.

Then Ariely introduced a disappearing door. The door that offered the lowest winnings gradually became smaller and disappeared, unless the participant clicked on it for at least one of their twelve clicks. This change led to people winning far less: they kept on clicking on the disappearing door just enough to keep it. Despite the door winning them almost nothing, they continued to click on it, even after the researchers displayed the average yield per door. And it didn't stop there. Even when people were able to bring the door back with a click, they continued to click on it and suffer the losses. What is it with disappearing options?

The final Concorde flights were the most sought-after in living memory. The closing down sales of the UK department store Debenhams drew large crowds, despite the shop having struggled for years. Now or never, last chance, closing sale, panic buying; one of the housefly effects behind this is FOMO, the fear of missing out. Tim and his wife regularly become stressed out when yet another lovely pop-up restaurant in Amsterdam is reaching its closing date and they haven't got around to eating there yet. They're better able to resist the limited-edition burgers of the big fast-food chains, but the irregularly available McRib draws hordes to McDonald's in America, because you never know how long it will be before it's back.* It makes sense that the opposite can also happen. When doubt about availability is removed, demand drops again. While Obama was president, American firearms enthusiasts were worried that he would take away their weapons, so they bought up pistols, guns and ammo in large quantities, and the industry enjoyed a (deadly) heyday. But then Trump came to power, a Republican with the support of the National Rifle

---

* See also the variable reward in chapter 2.

Association. Keen shooters of the nation breathed a sigh of relief and instantly stopped buying so much weaponry. Famous names such as Remington and Smith & Wesson ran into deep financial difficulties as a result, a phenomenon that came to be known as the Trump Slump.

> **Try this at home**
>
> What do you do about it? How do you swat away the sticky suggestion that you 'might regret it'? Ariely demonstrated that practice doesn't help, and nor does providing people with information beforehand. But there are ways. Say you want to buy a house but aren't sure what the market's going to do, and you're worried about rotten foundations.
>
> 1. List the costs of *not choosing*. How much time are you spending on the decision now? What's the consequence of doing nothing? What are the different potential scenarios and what are the chances of each?
>
>> (... if I don't buy a house now, the rent I'll have to pay will rise by X percent each year. In five years' time I'll have spent this much on rent...)
>
> 2. Then list the consequences of making the wrong decision. What would you need to do to reverse that choice? Be specific and as comprehensive as you can.
>
>> (... if I buy the wrong house now, I'll have to pay stamp duty twice...)

3. Predict your emotions in each case. Assign them a score. Note that you intuitively tend to overestimate the intensity of future emotions: you become accustomed to both improvements and deteriorations faster than you think. So reduce your predicted emotion by a factor of three.

4. Compare. There's a good chance that option 1 is a big disappointment and that option 2 turns out far better than expected, and that your predicted emotions in 3 are not as intense as feared.

Will they, won't they?

How does the combination of uncertainty, money and not being able to decide work out in practice? Think of a spot swarming with flies, where people often spend money without knowing precisely how much they're spending in total. Yep, the supermarket. Unless you shop with one of those self-scan devices, the final total at the till is often a surprise. If you have 20 quid on you, it takes considerable calculating capacity to stay within the limit. Wouldn't it be handy to have your running total projected on your shopping trolley? It sounds so practical that you wonder why shopping trolleys still don't all have a simple scanner or calculator.

What do you reckon, would you spend more or less with a screen at the front of your trolley or basket? Turns out it depends on whether you have a budget in mind.[10] Budget shoppers equipped with a tablet on average spent more (42 dollars) than those without (34 dollars). The feedback made them less uncertain as to the total price, so they didn't feel the need to build in as much of a margin. They then spent the margin on 'extras', in particular additional branded products. People without a budget, on the other hand, spent less when they were continually reminded of the price: those without a tablet spent 55 dollars, whereas those with one spent 41 dollars, mainly due to replacing premium products with own brands in the latter group.

So it seems feedback on the total price has a variable effect, depending on what type of customer you are, but in this case both kinds of customer were better off in their own way. In online shops there's often a product counter at the top of your screen, rather than a total price. It means Amazon loses out on potential purchases from budget shoppers who would happily spend to their limit, but don't because they're uncertain.

> **Feedback in your pocket**
>
> Ten years ago an MIT lab designed a living wallet. It came in three versions: one quivered when you used your credit card; another became thicker the more you had in your current account; and the best design had a hinge that became harder to open the closer you came to using up all your money. We're talking proper 'sludge' here. They made resistance beneficial.

Do we really need that feedback to stay within our budget? It certainly doesn't do anything to improve the shopping experience. Another way of avoiding that financial uncertainty is prepaying, or at least fixing a price in advance, for instance by going all-inclusive. Most travellers know that they pay a bit much for that wristband. Some try to compensate by getting everything they can from the buffet. Seinfeld also weighed in on this topic: 'No one would go into a restaurant and say to the waiter, "I'll have a yoghurt parfait, spare ribs, waffle, meat pie, crab leg, four cookies and an egg white omelet."' Yet at a prepaid buffet people eat as if they were sentenced to death and permitted to choose their final meal. Even people who eat more modestly gain extra enjoyment from their holiday by avoiding financial surprises after the event. It's a far more pleasant experience than waiting in a sweat for the final judgment of the supermarket till!

Uncertainty is suffering. Imagine a friend messages you, 'I might have a ticket to that sold-out concert for you.' Are you more or less happy after reading it? Many people are less so. Before the message the world seemed simple: you weren't going to the concert, that's the way it was. Now two possible worlds exist: one in which you're looking forward to a great night out, and another in which you got your hopes up for nothing and are left bitterly disappointed at home.

But sometimes uncertainty feels good. The American trend for baby showers is making its way to the UK, yet many parents still explicitly ask the sonographer not to reveal the child's gender on the ultrasound. That way the parents can spend half a year... well, what exactly? Looking forward to two possible outcomes? What's going on here? What's the difference from the previous context? Uncertainty is only pleasant when you see both outcomes as positive – parents probably don't opt to wait longer in uncertainty if they have a strong preference, as that turns uncertainty back into suffering.

But some certainty can be *overkill*. Popcorn isn't any tastier when a large calorie label announces how many extra calories you'll need to burn if you eat your way through the entire bag.[11*]

---

[*] Cass Sunstein (one of the two authors of *Nudge*) wrote proudly to a friend that the American Food and Drug Administration had finally made information on calorie counts in restaurants and cinemas compulsory. His friend wrote back, 'Cass ruined popcorn!'

Pain and how to turn it into gain

That's the kind of painful information people are willing to pay not to see: the **ostrich effect**[12] – think of the shocking images on cigarette packets, which few smokers stop to look at closely. People differ enormously in whether they find negative information pleasant or painful. Think of the calories. Are you someone with little self-control? Then you probably just find it annoying, because you're going to eat the whole bag anyway, but will enjoy it less as a result. If you have a little more self-control, you don't perceive it as painful, but there's a good chance you'll buy a smaller bag of popcorn. That's a shame, of course, because the calorie count is really there for the group lacking self-control. What's going wrong with that group lacking self-control[13] that makes information hurt? The clear numbers deprive you of your 'ethical room for manoeuvre', or worse, your philosophy of life, and losing something hurts. That's why we close our eyes, sometimes almost literally. How else does that artisanal butcher get away with the life-size piglet smilingly recommending the rumps of its brothers and sisters?

> It's sometimes perplexing to see how far we're prepared to go to protect our philosophy of life against new information.[14] A group of people, some of them climate deniers, were presented with the predicted temperature rise for the year 2100. Half of them were then given good news ('fortunately there are significant indications that it won't be as bad as anticipated'); the other half received only bad news ('and there's worse'). They were then asked whether they believed in climate change and how much they thought that the temperature would rise in 2100. Those who had said they didn't believe in climate change, of course, barely responded to being told it would be

> worse than they thought, but when they received good news, they instantly adjusted their estimation. Somehow that sort of makes sense: good news fits into their belief system, as they already thought things would be fine. But the odd thing was, of the people who said they believed in climate change the most, those who received bad news updated their estimations for 2100 even more drastically (4 degrees warmer in 2050!) than those who had received good news. Or rather, although the news was bad for humanity, they readily believed it because it confirmed their existing conviction. Your philosophy of life clearly outweighs the climate.

In this chapter you've seen how people avoid pain, regret and uncertainty, along with the houseflies that accompany them. You encountered the endowment effect and now you understand why sellers and buyers on eBay so often get into conflict. When it came to loss aversion, you may have been reminded of the clutter in your loft that you can't let go of. And when we described defensive decisions, you probably recognised a situation in which you opted for 'definitely no disappointment' instead of holding out for the very best possible outcome. The ostrich effect, the unwillingness to receive unpleasant information, may have been familiar too. You can actually use these houseflies in your daily life. First of all, be aware that others may be playing on your loss aversion. In order to stay sharp, it's a good idea to reread this chapter regularly. Tip: avoid being left without a copy if you lose this one, or it gets stolen or soaked in coffee! Order a spare now, it'll give you peace of mind. Okay, we don't suppose you'll fall for that. Nevertheless, pay attention if you see this housefly hovering over a heap of unnecessary insurance policies and warranties, and

Pain and how to turn it into gain

keep an eye out for opportunities to apply them. For instance, compare these emails:

> 'Dear Parents, it's time for the voluntary donation to the school. Please do contribute, as this makes school trips possible and the children always very much enjoy them.'

> 'Dear Parents, it's time for the voluntary donation to the school. Please do contribute, as otherwise our children will lose out on the school trips they so enjoy.'

This housefly doesn't always work, but we know which we'd send. A final warning: before releasing this fly into your home, always consult the words on ethics at the end of this book!

> The social fly likes to follow groups, leaders and norms.

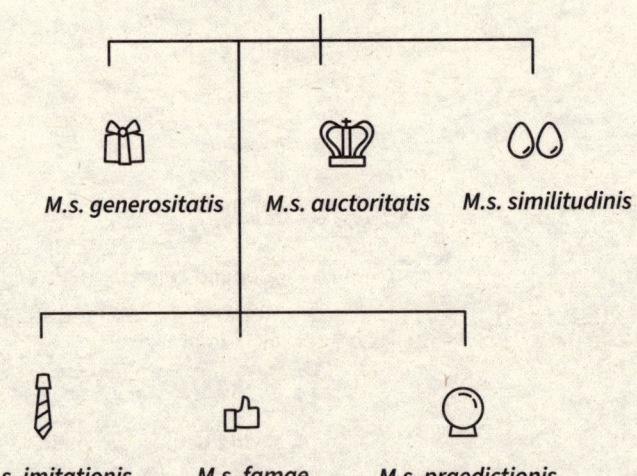

Chapter 4

Conforming – are you doing it too?

Musca socialitatis or 'social fly'

Subspecies: *M.s. generositatis* (altruism), *M.s. auctoritatis* (authority), *M.s. similitudinis* (familiarity), *M.s. imitationis* (social norms), *M.s. famae* (reputation), *M.s. praedictionis* (game theory).

This housefly is a social animal. Swarms are bound by strict rules and a clear hierarchy, with members following the lead of the flies with the most authority. The solidarity on display is impressive but can backfire too.

Application: the mere suggestion of a fly having been somewhere can attract new flies. A recent mutation of the *M.s. imitationis* is the *M.s. FOMO*.

Imagine you're in a foreign city, looking for a fun place to go clubbing. You've got two options. One has a long queue and a stony-faced bouncer, who will grudgingly admit a group of people every so often. The other has a tout on the door: 'Come on in! This is a great place! First drink on the house!' A rational being would choose the second establishment: no wait time, no risk of a humiliating rejection and free alcohol to boot! But you probably join the queue. Why? Is it the atmosphere, the music or something else that makes it the better club? No, all you have to go on at this point is that queue. And it's enough for you to spend an hour shivering on a street corner.

Social animals

Society may feel individualistic, but human beings are social animals at heart. It explains why social houseflies have such a strong influence on our behaviour. Just look at that club.

You could create a detailed Excel spreadsheet listing all the pros and cons of each club, but the night would be over by the time you were done. Thankfully, your brain has a handy tactic for uncertain situations like this: do what most other people do. This may seem irrational, until you remember that this rule of thumb can be very effective. Admittedly, what the majority does isn't always best (hello fast-food chains!), but it's rarely a huge disappointment either. So when you're unsure of something, following the crowd is an excellent risk-avoidance strategy. Your distant forebears

Conforming – are you doing it too?

sensed as much: while everybody is fleeing a tiger, you *could* go and stroke it, but it's not exactly conducive to survival.

When in doubt, do what everyone else is doing and you'll be fine. It's called **social proof** or the **bandwagon effect**. You don't even need to see those others, as long as you can infer what they did. Businesses love to deploy this housefly. Think of the pop-ups on online shopping sites telling you about their 'best-selling item' and that 'ten others are viewing this room now'. *50,000,000 Elvis Fans Can't Be Wrong* was the title of an album by The King, and for many years sitcoms used laughter tracks and live studio audiences to get viewers to laugh. While that's no longer fashionable, during the pandemic football matches that were played behind closed doors were shown with canned cheering, as it made the experience more compelling for viewers at home.

That nightclub queue boasts another housefly: scarcity. Lots of people want to gain entry, but not everybody gets in! So those choosing this club haven't just made the right decision, they may even get to show off afterwards. Scarcity confers status: we're in, they're out. (This little fly is related to the **snob effect**: when more people have something, it brings down the value of that object.) That scarcity is desirable is illustrated by the Michelin-starred restaurant that you have to book a full six months in advance, and by the rush on H&M as soon as a famous designer drops a limited-edition collection. The merest hint of scarcity is effective. News reports warning of stockpiling are self-fulfilling prophecies: everybody is going to pick up an extra roll of toilet paper in case other people start hoarding and they end up with nothing. A supermarket announcing that soft drinks are limited to four bottles per person will see an instant boost in sales.[1] And then there's the clever ploy of having posters urging customers to be patient a week prior to the launch of a new product. It suggests a hype, and your head will be buzzing with that.*

---

* Tim neither confirms nor denies applying such techniques in campaigns.

The Housefly Effect

Bestseller lists are predicated on the same principle. Books on that list sell even better: the **bestseller effect**.* Now I hear you thinking: those publications are objectively good. That's true, at least in part, but luck plays a big role too. In 2006, three researchers set up an online music store with unknown songs and invited 7,192 participants to download tracks.[2] These people were able to see previous listener favourites. The beauty of the experiment lay in the fact that there were eight subgroups, each with its own chart. The ultimate top ten turned out to be heavily influenced by what was downloaded at the start, an effect compounded by algorithms that recommended the popular titles more often: again, the **bestseller effect**.

There's a flipside to this story. Cast your mind back to that other club at the start of this chapter. That sad, empty place is home to our housefly's ugly little brother. Nobody wants to go somewhere that's empty, whether it's a nightclub, a restaurant or a department store. Not only does it feel uninviting, but surely there must be a reason why nobody wants to be there? Popularity breeds more popularity, emptiness more emptiness, in the same way that rubbish strewn across the street attracts even more rubbish.[3]

This can have unintended consequences, for instance when campaigns highlight the scale of a problem. 'Thousands of motorists run red lights every year!' 'Recycling at an all-time low!' 'Hundreds of bus drivers at the receiving end of violence!' The public sector loves these types of campaigns, not least because they show the organisation behind them addressing a Major Problem. But, more often than not, they achieve the exact opposite of what you'd hoped for. In all these cases, the undesirable behaviour has been made to look normal. If that many people are doing it... There's now a good chance that instead of curbing this conduct you're encouraging it.

---

* So thank you, dear reader. And why not buy *The Housefly Effect* as a gift for someone else?

Conforming – are you doing it too?

Project Excellent Together

You can test this in your own workplace by asking your colleagues to contribute to your project – ideas, information or just a date when they're free to attend a meeting. But weeks pass and your mailbox remains empty. Time for a strongly worded email, something along these lines:

> *Dear colleagues,*
>
> *Two months ago, I asked for your input regarding Project Excellent Together. To date, I've received 1 (one!) response. Not exactly excellent! Please submit your suggestions by tomorrow at the latest, because we're in this together.*

That'll teach 'em, right? Erm... remember that housefly earlier? We feel comfortable in the presence of lots of others. A collective sigh of relief now ripples through the office. *Phew, nobody else is taking part. Glad I'm not that one loser who wasted time on this.* You've turned your beautiful project into an empty, unappealing club. What's more, you've deployed the wrong housefly: people may no longer want to chip in for fear of being seen as weird and getting ostracised.

We wouldn't recommend you stand outside the meeting room and refuse entry to your colleagues, like that famous bouncer at Berlin techno club Berghain, the one with the intimidating face tattoos. But you can certainly borrow elements from the snob principle. Why not try an email like this next time:

> Dear colleagues,
>
> Project Excellent Together is well on track. More and more*
> co-workers are sharing their opinions. Although we'd love
> to include everyone, there's a limit to how many ideas we
> can take on board. So if you haven't provided your input
> yet, you have until the end of this week!

Normal's the norm

Do you remember the 'normcore' trend from a few years back, when young men donned white socks and young women wore comfortable mom jeans? *Core* was short for *hardcore* – very tough – and by adopting this style you showed that you really couldn't care less about other people's opinions. Finally, normal had become hip. What a refreshing trend! In reality, people have always wanted to be normal. We're hard-wired that way, if only to avoid our biggest fear: social exclusion.

> When Eva moderates workshops for civil servants, she'll
> sometimes begin the day with a game. Some of the
> participants are invited to step out into the corridor,
> where they're given directions. Back in the room,
> everybody starts throwing balls in groups of three.

---

* We started with zero, now we have one: technically, that's more. Advertising creative Tim doesn't think this is misleading. Scientist Eva agrees, as long as you're not actively telling falsehoods (she'd remove 'and more') and people don't feel lied to. Otherwise they'll never trust you again, and that would ruin your next housefly experiment...

Conforming – are you doing it too?

> After one minute, the 'insiders' carry out their instructions and exclude a few of the players – they're no longer thrown any balls, while everyone else carries on. That hurts, whether you see it coming or not. Even those who've read about these kinds of experiments underestimate how hurtful social exclusion is and how uncomfortable it feels to exclude someone. This ball game gives you first-hand experience of one of humankind's strongest drivers: the desire to belong.

Being different is so painful that people are even prepared to modify their convictions in order to fit in. It's not even as if it takes pressure from a huge crowd. Back in 1951 psychologist Solomon Asch concluded that three people saying the same thing will nearly always* be backed up by a fourth – even when their claims are patently untrue. He hired students to claim in front of unsuspecting participants that two lines were the same length when this was evidently nonsense. Two actors didn't have enough persuasive power to convince someone, but 75 percent of all subjects would conform at least once if more than two people made nonsensical claims. So in order to stand your ground in a group discussion, even when you're obviously right, you must be able to endure the pain of exclusion.[4†]

This fear of exclusion also impinges on career choice. At the

---

* But beware: this experiment is based on the answers of only fifty participants, and they were lied to.

† It gets scarier: most of the incorrect information we receive these days is generated by algorithms and knowledge-based systems. This has prompted other researchers, seventy years on from Asch's study, to examine whether we're equally susceptible to blatantly wrong advice doled out by an algorithm (of the '2 + 2 = 5' variety). Sadly, in this situation too we cave in and, against our better judgement, choose the wrong answer. Even in encounters with AI, we experience pressure to conform.

start of 2019, the Tacoma Police Department in Washington State sought to diversify its workforce but didn't get very far. Anyone who wasn't a young white male dropped out during the recruitment process, despite repeated assurances that women and minorities were more than welcome. Often, all applicants would be white before an initial selection had even taken place. That's when the Behavioural Insights Team[5] came up with a new strategy that acknowledged that individuals from a minority background don't identify with the average police officer. They advertised on Facebook, showing a black man, a white woman and an Asian man, captioned 'You belong here'. The number of applications from non-white males quadrupled. Apparently, people needed visual affirmation that they fitted the mould and wouldn't be excluded.

Us versus them

A **social norm** is a rule of behaviour that people are expected to conform to in a particular situation, in a particular group. Sometimes norms are made explicit. A pastor or imam can explain the correct way of interacting with the opposite sex, an etiquette guide specifies what to do with your napkin if you need to leave the table to go to the lavatory between courses,* while a columnist may tell you what words to avoid at work. Such norms reinforce cohesion within your own ranks (the in-crowd) while widening the gap between you and the rest (the outsiders). Nothing boosts team spirit like getting together to persecute heathens, thumbing your nose at the plebs or snickering at the manager who's always talking about 'circling back'. Other norms are less explicitly defined and are often learned subconsciously by observing the behaviour of people in your group and the reactions to those who deviate from the rules.

---

* You place it to the left of your plate – in case you were wondering. And, for heaven's sake, don't refer to that lavatory as a toilet.

But sometimes you jump to the wrong conclusion, based on what you see. During the coronavirus pandemic you couldn't really tell how many people obeyed lockdown rules and quarantined when necessary – those who did weren't out and about. But images of rule-breakers going to the beach in droves did make it into the papers.

The truly important, kick-ass norms in society tend to govern one and the same thing: self-interest versus the common good. Teaching us the value of making personal sacrifices, they are the theme of literally every single superhero film. Their key message? Putting yourself above all else is something villains do. A recent example is flight shame, the awareness that long-haul travel is nothing to brag about. It's a typical social norm: it polices normal behaviour, is confined to certain circles and involves weighing up self-interest against the common good (a nice holiday versus climate change). Many airlines capitalise on their customers' guilt by inviting them to offset the carbon emissions in the form of a few new trees. Do this, share it on social media and you're all good.

Chocolates for your colleagues

Here's a way to measure whether being considerate is the norm in your workplace. Take a box of chocolates into a meeting, but make sure you buy too few; aim to have two-thirds of the total number of people present. Before you pass them round, tell everyone:

- how many chocolates you have;

- that everyone is allowed to help themselves to 0, 1 or 2 (please note: ask them to jot down how many they intend to take);

> - and that you'll take all the chocolates home again if your colleagues claim more than you have.
>
> Fun fact: in most groups, people somehow manage to get it just right. Funner fact: bosses usually take two. They always have a reason of course: 'for my intern/husband/daughter'. Even so.

In many cases, what people *think* ought to be done isn't the same as what most of them do. The two are diametrically opposed in some situations, for instance when corruption and crime are rife. What carries more weight for a novice coke dealer: the descriptive norm ('what my friends are doing') or the injunctive norm ('what I ought to do')? There's often a discrepancy between what you think you ought to do and what you're actually doing (like more exercise and less doom scrolling on your phone). By and large, the visible behaviour of others will be the deciding factor, rather than what you believe is appropriate. There goes another young coke dealer.

It's no surprise. What others do is something you can see, but what they think is much harder to gauge. An insight into this can be nothing short of revolutionary, as a study from Saudi Arabia demonstrates.[6] Some women there work outside the home but most don't, as their husbands object to it. That was the perceived idea anyway, but research showed a different picture. The husbands themselves are fine with their wives working, but think *others*, such as neighbours, would disapprove. In reality, unbeknownst to both parties, the neighbours were equally open to it. The researchers decided to inform a random selection of the men that others were also okay with working women. And guess what? Shortly afterwards many of them registered their wives with a job matching service, and four months later a sizable number of these women were happily employed. It illustrates the way that misconceptions about social norms can make or break whole societies (and marriages).

The norms they are a-changing

How can you establish, or transform, a social norm? One way of doing this is by turning a change in the norm into a norm in its own right. Three American scholars tested this in their own backyard, or in their university canteen, to be precise. Some 80 percent of customers would order a lunch containing meat, and queue, on average, for five minutes to do so. The researchers handed questionnaires to everybody waiting in line. Version A mentioned how many Americans had reduced their meat consumption (three out of ten); version B noted how many had *started* to cut back on meat (curiously enough, also three out of ten). So the two questionnaires were identical, save for a couple of words. But the effect on people's orders was huge: the group that read about others having *started* to eat less meat ordered twice as many vegetarian lunches (34 percent) than their 'been doing this a while' fellow-customers.[7] It goes to show that you can modify a norm without lying – simply by highlighting tiny changes. Speaking of a housefly effect.

Cast your mind back to those chocolates for your colleagues. That situation in which you're tasked as a group not to claim too many, even though you'd love to take two for yourself, is known as a social dilemma. They're quite common and cover everything from overfishing to speeding. When people are presented with one in an experiment (which generally doesn't revolve around chocolate, but around joint investments), you'll find that many of the participants are considerate in the first round and take decisions that are in the interests of the community as a whole – at least in the Netherlands, where it's the norm to trust one another. That said, every so often Eva sees groups in the lab in Amsterdam where, from the outset, nobody puts any money in the collective kitty. Because, let's face it, you're not some kind of sucker (officially known as the **sucker effect**).[8] On average, about a third of participants are such *freeloaders*. But once they've played the game a few times, most people conclude that selfishness pays off, not least because it prevents others from taking advantage of their generosity. In the long run, the norm to be considerate breaks down.

So how come we appear to have mastered quite a few social dilemmas in our day-to-day lives? We queue at the checkout, cough in our elbow and flush public toilets, in part because we tend to cooperate conditionally, even in groups:[9] when you see someone else put a deposit down, you're prepared to do the same. That's true for about 50 percent of people and is reinforced by social norms: it's simply not done to jump the queue when others are patiently waiting their turn. When these norms aren't powerful enough, we're very good at working out alternative mechanisms to keep people in line. But while penalising deviant behaviour can be very effective* (think of speeding fines – see chapter 7), it can also be a bit risky. Would you have the courage to tell a businesswoman who's on her phone that she's in the quiet coach?

Valentine's Day and the shower drain

Thankfully, having a stern word with offenders isn't the only solution; you can simply exclude anyone who doesn't cooperate. This may sound like something you'd never do, but think about it: our lives are punctuated by physical and financial transactions between strangers, and most of them pass off successfully. For instance, eBay had over 132 million active users worldwide in

---

* Herrmann, Thöni and Gächter (2008) write at length about people in Athens, Istanbul and Muscat meting out more punishment than most Europeans. Curiously enough, they tend to punish the highest contributors.

2023, while over 448 million nights and experiences were booked on Airbnb that year. Users of both these platforms, as well as nearly every other online marketplace, can see how the other party's previous activities were rated. At first glance, this looks like a great idea, but in the early days, all kinds of unintended houseflies could be seen buzzing around. Do you remember when Airbnb guests were allowed to post their review before the host? What did you do back then – give your honest opinion about the shower drain and risk the host hitting back at you? Of course not. That self-censorship suited Airbnb only too well, as it pushed up the average number of stars awarded. But as rating inflation struck, people lost confidence in the system. After consulting experts, Airbnb decided to withhold reviews until both parties had had their say. It's like Valentine's Day: when you post your card, you don't know whether the other person likes you too. The withholding helped – a little, anyway. Because let's face it, if you're a strategic host, you're never going to say anything nasty, because your reactions are public. Future guests may well be checking whether you're the irascible type!

Now imagine you're the CEO of Airbnb. How do you tackle these problems?[10]* You look at other platforms and see that they allow people to edit or retract their evaluation later on. But that opens a whole new can of worms. As a reader of this book, you'll understand that it unlocks the door to abuse. Users can systematically dole out bad reviews and then negotiate a solution with the other party. This kind of blackmail is common on Yelp, with diners threatening to post one-star reviews unless they're offered freebies.

Luckily, not many people are that dishonest. Still, figures show that retracting reviews undermines user confidence, which could ultimately bring the whole system down. **Reputations** are worth

---

* What would your ideal marketplace look like? Michael Luca's 'Designing Online Marketplaces' is a very readable 'economists' toolkit' about building trust and reputation mechanisms into platforms.

a lot of money. Reputable sellers can charge 16 percent more for their product than comparable ones without a good name. It turns out that potential buyers and guests are very susceptible to information about vendors. But this has drawbacks too: African-American hosts saw a 12 percent drop in income when they added a photo to their profile.[11]*

Social signals everywhere

If you want to belong, you have to adhere to social norms – and to be seen to be doing so; anyone displaying antisocial behaviour will ultimately get kicked out of the group. There's just one problem: claiming that you're extremely socially capable gives out the wrong signals and makes you look like you're on an ego trip. Sadly, the opposite, humble bragging, doesn't work either: people who boast by being self-deprecating – 'My worst quality is being a perfectionist, it's terrible!' – are seen as less competent, less likeable and even likely to get less done.[12]† Tricky! Then what are you to do? Luckily, there are other, more casual ways of conveying that you're socially sensitive, such as raising money for a good cause, marching against pollution, taking on the role of treasurer of the sports club or starting an online petition. By helping others you may even (perhaps unintentionally) help yourself. Being known as a valuable member of society assures you of the group's protection *and* gives

---

* Part of the appeal of Uber, the taxi app, lies in the fact that this type of discrimination is impossible, because the algorithm determines pricing based on ride requests, driver availability and ratings.

† How would you actually research this? Three American scholars asked subjects to choose between humble-bragging sentences ('Oh yeah, so embarrassing, everybody says I'm the spitting image of that film star' and 'It's so time-consuming when everybody turns to you for advice') and straight-up boastful ones ('I'm good at chairing meetings' and 'I'm the fastest runner in my age group') and select the statements that described them best. Subsequently, other participants got to hand out money on the basis of these choices. The humble braggers didn't do so well and received a lot less than the braggarts.

you a competitive edge over others on the dating market. It goes some way towards explaining why evolution continues to produce sociable altruists.

Moral immunity

However, sometimes things take a wrong turn and virtue signalling ends up trumping real action. Facebook activism is a case in point: it feels good, but how many people will actually get into a rubber dinghy to stop whalers after seeing your 'save the whales' post? In fact, your willingness to spring into action can decrease precisely because you've already sent a signal, as if you have an inner voice whispering: 'I just shared that impressive video about the plastic soup in the ocean, so my reputation is pretty solid and I've done enough for now. Yes, ma'am, I'd like a plastic bag!' This is a housefly that's clearly heading in the wrong direction.

Scientists call this the **moral licensing effect**. Just like children in a game of tag can't be 'it' straight after tagging someone, you have moral immunity after a good deed. For a while, you feel less susceptible to a reputational setback, which may explain why so many morally superior leaders and activists struggle to practise what they preach. Remember that craze for awareness ribbons, bracelets and tote bags from around the turn of the millennium? It was a popular way of showing that you championed a particular cause but, while those visible signs of support were on the rise, regular donations actually fell. The reasons for this may be varied – maybe the younger generation doesn't like such commitments – but to us it shows signs of moral licensing: you're wearing that yellow bracelet, so your job here is done.

Sometimes social behaviour becomes so competitive that the beneficiary starts to feel uncomfortable. Perhaps you've been on the receiving end of this after hurting yourself at a party. When you've got a bloody nose, being the centre of attention is the last thing you want, but your mishap is an opportunity for other party-goers to show themselves at their most socially concerned. They're falling over themselves to help! Researchers have identified something similar in a bird species, the wonderfully named Arabian Babbler. Its members appear to compete for the 'privilege' of selflessly helping the group by standing sentinel,[13] possibly to improve their social status. It's known as **competitive altruism**. We're reminded of this study every time we see celebrities trying to outdo each other in speaking up for a good cause.

Big Brother is watching us?

What others think of us influences our behaviour, even when they're not around. If you've ever felt ashamed of an ugly thought you'd never share with anyone, then you'll know how deeply conditioned we are to look at ourselves through other people's eyes. The mere suggestion that we're being watched puts us on our best behaviour. It's something religious leaders drew on long before it became the subject of systematic analysis by scientists: the higher power sees everything! The public sector isn't averse to this tactic either. British citizens who refused to pay speeding fines did cough up when the penalty notice included photographic evidence of the traffic offence.* Also in the UK, in the London borough of Woolwich, vandalism dropped by some 24 percent after children's faces were painted onto shop-front roller shutters.†
Eyes and faces hold a special place in our brains. Have you ever spotted a face in a car, the clouds or an electrical socket? It's called pareidolia. Part of your brain is constantly on the lookout for faces. Subconsciously, we're keen to know where we might find other living beings *and* what they're looking at. This mechanism has

---

* The authorities in France stopped providing these images, because they clearly revealed the cars' occupants and with it lots of cheating partners.
† The study was titled 'Babies of the Borough'.

been identified in very young children and is known as the eye direction detector (EDD). This too can be 'hacked'. In an experiment, researchers increased charity donations by nearly half by sticking googly eyes on the collection box! However, analysis of numerous studies of this phenomenon has shown that the effect is small[14] – unless the eyes in question are female. In that case, men feel compelled to donate more.[15] And here's a tip: if you decide to include a face on the poster advertising your office party, make sure the eyes are looking at your text or you risk directing the viewer's attention to the blank wall beside it.

> The final and most bizarre way in which signals function as houseflies is known as self-signalling. Sometimes you have to convince yourself that you're a decent human being by behaving in a certain way. In his book *The (Honest) Truth About Dishonesty*,[16] Dan Ariely described an astounding housefly effect: the **what the hell effect**. Ariely gave subjects a counterfeit Prada bag and then tested whether they answered questions more or less truthfully. Guess what happened? They became less honest, as though they were thinking, 'What the hell, I'm already pulling a fast one by flashing a fake designer bag, so what's one more lie?' People like to think of themselves as decent human beings, but when their actions suggest otherwise, their self-image crumbles and they feel there's less reason to be well-behaved.*

---

* Eva had a first-class 'what the hell' experience when she was driving down a busy motorway during lockdown and read the 'stay home' advice. Already a lawbreaker, she later put the bins out after curfew.

Authority and rectal ear drops

Please join us in a thought experiment. Eva's doctoral research suggests it can be an extremely useful thing to do. Picture the following two scenarios.

> Scenario 1. You're in hospital for tests. A man in a brightly coloured tracksuit examines you and prescribes strong medication.
>
> Scenario 2. You're in hospital for tests. A man in a pristine white coat examines you and prescribes strong medication.

In which scenario would you be a good patient and take those pills? And when would you be more inclined to ask for a second opinion?

The thought experiment gave you a taster of the **white-coat effect**. You'd probably be more critical of the tracksuited physician. This is one heck of a housefly, because what does the white coat really mean? Clothes maketh the man, as the saying goes, but they really don't make him any more knowledgeable. Yet subconsciously, you experience this attire as a symbol of authority. That's why people are prepared to accept more from doctors (or actors) wearing white coats, in experiments as well as in real life. An infamous example is that of the nurse who received written instructions from a physician: the ear drops were to be given in the right ear, or, as the notes said, 'R. ear'. However, he read it as 'rear' and unquestioningly administered the drops rectally. Some people seem to abandon all common sense as soon as an authority enters the picture. While this example may be comical, it gets a lot more serious in the case of 'captainitis'. It's the phenomenon whereby co-pilots sometimes keep following the flight captain's instructions, against their better judgement and with devastating consequences, as evidenced by black-box recordings.

Conforming – are you doing it too?

Now I hear you thinking: medicine and aviation are so complex that you have no choice but to put your trust in an expert. Then let's look at the effect of a blue uniform. In a very different context, its impact is no less powerful. Experiments have shown that people are systematically more compliant when they receive instructions from individuals who look like police officers or security guards.[17] They even obey 'orders' to hand a stranger some cash for the parking meter! Going one better is the **red sneakers effect**: people who defy sartorial expectations, such as a CEO wearing red trainers, can end up projecting even more status and competence. They're seemingly so good, they get away with it. But, like the doctor in the tracksuit, this is an exception rather than the rule, and it probably works better in the creative industries than it does in operating theatres. Research into tattoos appears to suggest as much: terrible for a doctor's credibility, good for that of a chef.*

Advertisers recognised the power of authority early on. Remember the old ads in which 'four out of five dentists recommend' a particular toothpaste? This reached its zenith, or nadir if you like, in the campaign for 'Dr. Dushkind' cigarettes: just what the doctor ordered. These days, brands position themselves more subtly. They may enlist a wealthy actor – if anyone knows luxury watches, it's him – or perhaps a man who's so buff and suave he has no trouble persuading teenage boys that the deodorant he promotes will captivate the ladies. And don't forget the plethora of quality marks in the supermarket, all claiming one and the same thing: certified by an authority. Likewise, language choice can lend authority via association with a country. Sports brands from Germany such as Adidas and Puma are less likely to use German slogans than car makers, as the likes of Volkswagen and Audi (*Das Auto*, *Vorsprung durch Technik*) can tap into the nation's reputation for technology.

---

* Scientist Eva certainly has far fewer than creative mind Tim.

Everybody's an authority now

The number of authorities is booming. Gone are the days when we'd have a go-to figure in a particular area (the priest, the doctor, the teacher). Instead, we have influencers on Instagram and experts giving their two pennies' worth on talk shows; the millennial who tells us what's trending on X, the crime reporter who makes sense of an attack and the successful DJ reviewing the latest tracks. All authorities in their own field. (Whether or not it's smart to take health advice from an Instagram model is another matter.) Maybe you can benefit from this effect too. The good news is that you don't need to don a white coat or a blue uniform to do so. Perhaps you already are an authority on something, be it in your social circle or at work, because you've been around the block a few times, you studied the subject at university or you clocked up a nice achievement once. Don't be modest; shout it from the rooftops! Of course, there are tricks to further accentuate your authority. Introduce an obscure bit of information with the words, 'as many people know...' Or else compliment colleagues of the same rank as you on their work. It's flattering, but also paints you as being in a position to judge: aka the authority.

We have a confession to make. Eva's doctoral research had nothing to do with thought experiments.* But we figured that by referencing her authority as a scientist, we'd get you to actually do the thought experiment with the differently dressed doctors. Did it work?

Game theory – putting yourself in someone else's shoes

On social media you click 'like' when you appreciate something. Simple. Or is it? Imagine a friend posts a toe-curling poem riddled

---

* On the contrary: participants were paid hard cash for all the experiments in Eva's thesis.

with clichés and typos. You don't mind liking it, if only to make him happy, but you know others will see your 'like' too. What if they think that you believe his poetry is genuinely good? You'd better not like it then! So people are more inclined to click 'like' when they think others will like the fact that they like something. Confused? The vertigo you're experiencing right now is known as *Theory of Mind*.

To illustrate this, John Maynard Keynes, the British economist and Nobel Prize winner, drew up an analogy between the economy and a beauty contest. He described an imaginary newspaper contest in which readers can win a prize by guessing which of the faces pictured is seen as the most beautiful. Your task then is not to vote for the woman you personally find the most irresistible, but to predict who's best-looking in the eyes of the majority. The stock market works in the same way, Keynes argued. The most attractive option isn't always the one with the most intrinsic value. A tiny, random change in price can have a huge housefly effect.

Beauty contest

You're sitting round a table with a group of people, and you're all asked to jot down a number between 0 and 100 on a piece of paper. The person closest to two-thirds of the average wins a cash prize. What number do you choose?

Write the number here: ____

This is an abstract variation on Keynes' beauty contest. If everybody lists a random number (zero-order players), the expected average will be 50, and you'd win the game with two-thirds of that, i.e. 33. (Is that what you put down? You're a first-order thinker.) But those who work out that most people will probably get to this stage are better off saying 22 (congratulations – you're working on the basis of second-order beliefs!). Keep reasoning like this and you'll conclude that 0 is the best possible answer. Not all players will follow this line of thought to its extreme conclusion, far from it, so in practice picking 0 won't give you the win. This game is therefore not just about your level of strategic thinking, but also about gauging other people's ability.

Not everybody can execute the same number of mental steps in this kind of situation. When first faced with this kind of exercise, an estimated fifth of all people will be level 0 thinkers, a third will reach level 1, a quarter level 2 and the remainder will take their reasoning even further.[18] In practice, somewhere between levels 1 and 2 ('I *know* that you're *guessing* what I'm *thinking*') tends to yield the best results. In fact, this level of strategising usually comes out on top in computer simulations. So if you're after lots of likes on social media, then do think it through, but don't bother asking what friends of friends of friends might like.

Life is full of beauty contests. Whether you want to be better prepared for salary negotiations, company takeovers or a game of Risk, it pays to put yourself in another person's shoes – up to a point. If the above test revealed that your strategic thinking could use a little boost, there's a solution. Research suggests that the Theory of Mind muscle can be trained[19] – and, surprisingly enough, not by studying maths but by reading literature. Mills and Boon won't cut it, though; people don't hone their skills by reading 'what went through her mind', but by actively putting themselves in someone else's place, which is what a quality novel asks of you. It's worth doing, because a little bit of Theory of Mind goes a long way.

Kindness is infectious

Picture a ball rolling up a hill. Just before it gets to the top, a cube pushes it back down again! But then a triangle positions itself underneath the ball and nudges it up, step by step, until it reaches the summit. It's an abstract tragedy, but here's the rub – even infants under the age of one would rather play with the triangle than with the 'mean' square.[20] In other words, empathy has enabled us to develop a kindness detector and that's good for cooperation.

> **Evolution of trust**
>
> If you'd like to know how we can hold onto kindness in this harsh world, have a look at The Evolution of Trust. In this online game you're a stick figure that decides whether or not to cooperate with others in different scenarios: when another person is kind to you first, at random moments or when you've just been given something by someone else. You compete with other stick figures: an idiot, a softy who lets others walk all over him, someone who gets under your skin by being nice one moment and sneaky the next. You get to see how your choices influence the group's behaviour: will the baddies gain the upper hand or will the good guys? It's addictive fun, because after a while you begin to recognise the negotiation strategies that your colleagues or kids use on you. Ten minutes in you can claim to have an insight into a notoriously complex piece of science: evolutionary game theory.

Reciprocity is one of the cornerstones of human civilisation. Love is a process of give and take, as is the effort put into joint projects, rounds in the pub and presents in relationships. When the balance tips, things start to go wrong. That's why we have a kind of internal spirit level to maintain this equilibrium. If that mate of yours always responds to your jokes with a hearty 'hahahahaha!', then you don't react with a single lukewarm smiley. Organisations take advantage of this with houseflies in the shape of gifts. A free toy with your groceries, an interesting article in your inbox, a mint with your restaurant bill. And these rewards are effective. An experiment revealed that waiters who came back with extra sweets received 21 percent more in tips.[21] A more extreme manifestation of this, an escalating reciprocity of sorts, can be found in Japanese society. On Valentine's Day, women buy chocolate for men. A month later, on 'White Day', these men are expected to triple the value of what they give in return. If you're looking for an opportunity to end the relationship, then confectionery of equivalent value will convey the message loud and clear.

Yet often enough, people give without expecting anything in return. The question is why. At first glance, kindness doesn't seem to be all that advantageous, so it's worth asking why evolution has produced so much altruistic behaviour. Economists such as Adam Smith thought that being nice to others simply feels good. You may know it as that **warm glow effect**[22]* when you buy a copy of the *Big Issue*.

Biologists have also been fascinated by this question. Charles Darwin himself believed that people come to each other's aid for purely calculating reasons.[23]† Of course, that's part of it: monkeys groom one another in the hope that the favour is returned, and

---

* Adam Smith is the man behind *The Invisible Hand*, a title that convinced 90 percent of the world's economists that the economy is some kind of universal hocus-pocus. But he did write some sensible things: 'How selfish soever man may be supposed, there are evidently some principles in his nature, which interest him in the fortune of others, and render their happiness necessary to him, though he derives nothing from it, except the pleasure of seeing it.' In other words: a 'warm glow' or a nice feeling.

† Charles Darwin wrote in *The Descent of Man*: 'In the first place, as the reasoning powers and foresight of the members became improved, each man would soon learn that if he aided his fellow-men, he would commonly receive aid in return.' In other words: we're calculating creatures, human beings. Ultimately, these two explanations lead to one and the same conclusion: evolutionary pressure has ensured that something that's usually good for gene survival feels nice too. Like sex.

it's the same mechanism we see at work among colleagues. I'll do this job for you now but expect you to cover my back next time. The exclusively human twist in the tale is 'indirect reciprocity: you help Eva, Tim helps you. You don't reciprocate directly, pay it back, but do something for someone else, i.e. you 'pay it forward'. In the tearjerker of the same name Haley Joel Osment comes up with the idea that if someone does you a favour, you should be nice to three random people. You don't expect anything from those strangers except that they, in turn, pay your gesture forward to others.

3.4 million Chinese people and the Luckiest Draw

Now the question, of course, is whether people pay it forward in the real world and not just in sentimental films. WeChat suggests we do. This Chinese version of WhatsApp allows users to transfer money. Yuan and colleagues of the Massachusetts Institute of Technology have done research into this fascinating use of the app.[24] People can select a group of contacts to give money to. These individuals then all receive *hongbao*, a 'red packet' or envelope with money, a custom that's also observed at Chinese weddings and New Year celebrations. Everybody in the group is given a *random* amount of the cash. The actual sum isn't made public, but the person receiving the most is named as the Luckiest Draw. It's been a huge hit: 3.4 million Chinese people sent each other the equivalent of more than 17 million pounds within the space of a year!

Because the Luckiest Draw is selected randomly, Yuan and her colleagues were able to study whether kindness is indeed infectious. Does somebody who receives more also give away more; in other words, do people 'pay it forward'? They certainly do. Individuals who are given money for no reason can, of course, keep it all. However, the researchers found that anonymous recipients redonate an average of 10 percent of what they receive via the same red envelope system. Since it doesn't benefit them in any way, it appears that they simply enjoy passing it on. That said, reputational considerations do come into play as well. The Luckiest Draw, whose name is made public, behaves differently. He or she gives away a little more: an average of 15 percent. So publicity has an impact on your generosity, whether consciously or not, and encourages you to give just that little bit more. Both mechanisms, pay it forward and 'rational' reciprocity, appear to be anchored in our social structure. The existence of the different routes is confirmed by neuroscientists, who have identified two separate neural pathways, one 'selfish', the other 'empathetic'.[25] Two reasons why we're kind to one another.

Our propensity to be kind hasn't done humanity any harm. Doing something for another without insisting on reciprocity has enabled us to work together in big groups without constantly keeping score of 'who's done what for whom'. It leaves us free to drain polders, have democratic elections and maybe even save the world from rising sea levels. Besides, it's something you can deploy strategically. Give somebody a finger – and who knows, they may reverse the saying and give *you* their whole hand. That digit is a typical housefly!

Are you a do-gooder?

What would you do? Would you give away money like the WeChat users, for instance via a neighbourhood app? It's a lovely gesture, but it does feel rather strange to hand money to a neighbour for no reason. But what if you'd received 55 pounds as the Luckiest Draw yesterday? Perhaps you'd show your appreciation by asking him or her

Conforming – are you doing it too?

over for coffee or by giving more *hongbao* envelopes to others. But here's the question: would you include that one antisocial neighbour on the list of recipients?

- Yes, to look magnanimous. Congratulations! You're a strategic do-gooder.

- Yes, because you think it may make him or her a nicer person. Hats off to you! You're a 'pay it forward' benefactor!

- No, he or she doesn't deserve it. Good for you! You're a 'tit for tat' strategist, keeping the neighbourhood (and, in the long term, humanity as a whole) on its toes, so the sociopaths don't take control.

It's time to put this lesson into practice, as there's bound to be something you want from a colleague. Start by doing him or her a small favour, like offering to fetch a coffee perhaps; it improves the chance that he or she will do something for you in return.* Small gestures can make a huge difference to the atmosphere in an office – and allow you to bask in your own 'warm glow'.

Now you've seen that human beings are immensely social animals, and that this produces incredibly potent housefly effects. Likewise, you've learned that you can harness the power of social proof to your advantage by showing that many (or more and more) people are doing what you want. You're probably going to steer clear of

---

* A very peculiar housefly effect is the reverse of this. Once you get someone to do something small for you, they'll be more inclined to do you a bigger favour afterwards.

negative social proof, because when you stress how common bad behaviour is, you normalise it and unwittingly encourage it. After all, you're aware that, deep down, people are extremely receptive to norms. We hope that this chapter has also given you a better understanding of why people are kind or altruistic: not only does it feel good but living in a society with considerate people brings all sorts of benefits. And being seen as generous is good for your reputation. So be nice! But do watch out for the **moral licensing effect**, that sense of 'moral immunity' when your internal compass momentarily falters. Who knows, perhaps you can see a way to boost your own authority too. Why not share what you've learned with others? For purely altruistic reasons, of course!

> The temporal fly looks no further than the end of its nose.

Musca temporis

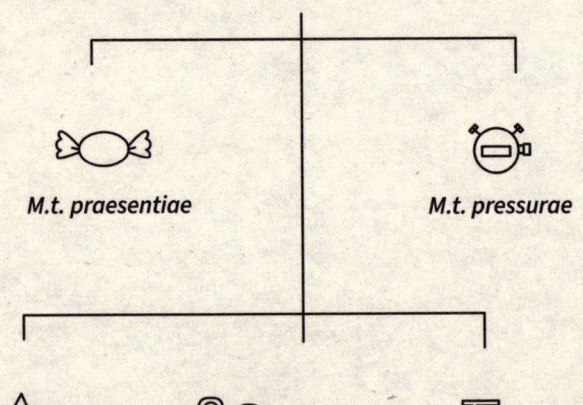

M.t. praesentiae

M.t. pressurae

M.t. culminis

M.t. consequentiae

M.t. procrastinationis

Chapter 5

Time has wings

Musca temporis **or 'temporal fly'**

Subspecies: *M.t. praesentiae* (present bias), *M.t. pressurae* (time pressure), *M.t. culminis* (peak), *M.t. consequentiae* (order), *M.t. procrastinationis* (procrastination)

Streamlined model, fleet of foot, arrives sooner than expected. Loud buzzing, commonly occurring, often in family contexts or in combination with *M. doloris*. Frequently spotted in work environments, around New Year's Eve and Black Friday, but also in hospitals and on holiday.

Management: tackle methodically with professional help.

Every decision is a prediction

Let's begin in childhood. In the most famous psychological experiment of the twentieth century, Walter Mischel offered four-year-olds a choice: would you like a marshmallow now, or two marshmallows after a twenty-minute wait?[1] There was the child, alone, eye to eye with the marshmallow. Some sat on their hands, others hid the sweet or turned their head away.* But most ate it after a second. This experiment has generated the tallest of tales. People even say it could be used to predict the children's earnings in later life. Such claims have all been debunked, but it's clear that Mischel was onto something. What was going on in the minds of those children? They clearly understood that two was more than one, but their prefrontal lobes were still insufficiently developed to resist. When the prefrontal lobe grows larger, it forms more connections with other regions, such as 'future-oriented thinking' in the hippocampus.[2] The stronger those connections, the more the owner values a reward in the future. But even fully developed prefrontal lobes rely on tricks to prevent them from forgetting their future selves.

For instance, yesterday Eva bought a pack of smoked trout,

---

* All strategies also employed by drug addicts to postpone use a bit longer.

discounted by 35 percent because it needed using within a day. Today she threw away the remaining half. That was a bit silly coming from a behavioural economist who has conducted research into food waste. She had fallen for the supermarket's trick, inducing her to buy something she couldn't finish.

How certain are you, when selecting a tasty treat, that you'll want precisely that a couple of days later? Positive? Most people are around 80 percent sure when they've chosen something to eat that they won't want to exchange it for something else.[3] But when push came to shove in an experiment, 55 percent of them chose something different in the end. In other words, Eva isn't the only overoptimistic fool. She was so sure of herself that she wasn't prepared to pay the full price for the option of being able to eat the trout a day later. The participants in the experiment were similarly unwilling to pay to be able to change their minds later. Of course the researchers don't call this trait stupidity, but 'overconfidence in future preferences for food'. That sounds like a workable message: don't take your own predictions about the future too seriously.

The same goes for the way we estimate our happiness in life. We overestimate the effect of big life events such as winning the lottery, a bucket-list holiday or a serious illness.* The bigger and more difficult it is to predict, the more we overestimate the magnitude and duration of the effect on our happiness. Of course it's an enormous blow to lose a breast, but after a year the happiness score of people with one breast is no different from that of others.[4] On the other hand, we underestimate how unhappy we'll feel about daily recurring chores like emptying the dishwasher and commuting.[5]

In short, we can't guess what our future self will think of something. That makes the temporal flies the stickiest of housefly families. Whether you're trekking through the jungle or standing

---

* See chapter 3 on loss aversion.

in the supermarket, the option that offers a small immediate reward is irresistible. Our brains are built to value rewards now (think marshmallows) far more than rewards in the future. That makes sense, because our distant ancestors who passed on their DNA to us had to grab whatever they could. Intermittent fasting on a strict schedule wasn't conducive to survival on the steppe, and their genetic legacy in our brain leads to odd mental derailments; we put off unpleasant things for too long (for instance, not saving enough). We systematically underestimate how long we'll take to do a task, and we allow our appreciation of a holiday to be determined by how pleasant the journey home was. *Musca prae-* *sentiae* can't be swatted away.

This chapter looks at the most prominent consequences of timing and our perception of time. We begin with... wait for it: the order of the next few paragraphs influences what you remember, so let's start with order effects. Then we'll reveal the bad news: our poor memory and prediction skills (think of Eva and the trout), and how decisions affect our happiness in life. Our failure to make sound predictions means we come up with poor plans, which go from bad to worse when we're stressed.

Fortunately we can do something about it. Factors such as the timing of a decision, how vividly we picture a situation and even the words we use to talk about the future all have a big impact on what we choose. Not to mention the many tricks you can use to protect yourself against this housefly – but we'll save them for last, because then they'll stick better.

Steered from start to finish: order matters

Architects pay close attention when they design the direction of walking routes in their buildings.* Marketers devise shopping

---

* That said, Eva used to work in an office where people could take the escalator routes in the supermarket and click routes in online shops. Sometimes they direct you with clear arrows and signs, as in the coronavirus pandemic, but more often with subtle housefly effects. Do you start out seeing the highest or lowest donation amount for a good cause? In the supermarket, why do you first pass the vegetables and then the crisps? And why do furniture stores with blue and yellow logos have cheap ice-cream on offer near the exit? These are all small, conscious **order effects** with a big influence on your choices – and their turnover.

Picture yourself walking around the supermarket of your choice. Whatever the colour of its logo, we know where you'll come in: near the fruit and veg. The big chains have studied these routes and layouts to the nth degree, so you can count on the order being lucrative. Because they sell more fresh goods this way? That too. Shoppers often simply grab anything prominent and within easy reach. That's all well and good, lots of healthy food, but in marketing circles you'll also hear a second explanation for why that fruit should go into your basket first. That super fresh bunch of carrots says, I've made a healthy start, and any possible guilt about your unhealthy lifestyle vanishes into thin air. So when you come to the crisps and speciality beers a little way along, you figure you might as well have them too. **Vicarious goal fulfilment** is the term for this effect.[6] With your fashionably knobbly organic apples, you're effectively buying a pardon for those fatty crisps. In the early 2000s, when McDonald's began to promote healthy products such as salads and spring water, sales of fast food actually increased. A neat order effect.

Supermarkets know you walk faster as you approach the till. Behind the scenes it's known as the 'checkout magnet'. Shops have been known to try to slow down the trolley with grooved tiles, but

---

to the fitness centre, something they did en masse. This was at the World Trade Center in The Hague: open all week to interested housefly tourists who would like to see the temporal fly in the wild.

in most cases the increased pace is desirable. The quicker you decide, the less time there is for you to suppress your impulses, which is why you're willing to pay more for a chocolate bar off the shelf at the till than for the same bar in a pack of five from the confectionery aisle. Those impulses at the end of a shopping trip also dovetail with another scientifically disputed but very recognisable phenomenon: **ego depletion**, the hypothesis that after resisting a great deal of temptation (turning down a lot of drinks) you kind of run out of willpower (and go crazy with the canapés). Perhaps your prefrontal lobe has blown its share of your brain's energy budget. The UK recently banned unhealthy products in 'impulse buy spots': only healthier products are now permitted near the exit and at the ends of aisles, which are particularly desirable positions for manufacturers. In online shops the same applies just before payment. Despite the ban, you can count on companies finding other ways to benefit from such order effects.

Outside work, order effects are often even stronger. Eva often eats out with a particular friend. The wine that tends to accompany those meet-ups makes it difficult to remember who paid last time, so they've come up with a system that's fair in principle: Eva tosses a coin and if it comes up heads she pays, if it's tails he does. Since the introduction of this system she's lost out seven times in a row, much to her friend's Schadenfreude. Eva was not amused with her dining companion taking such pleasure in her bad luck. Exemplifying the way anger tends to spur people on to take greater risks,[7] Eva suggested going to a more expensive restaurant the next time. It's an old casino trick: always at least double your stakes, then at some point you're sure to break even.

Well, Eva wouldn't be the only loser to fall into this trap. Aside from anger, losing a competition can encourage people to raise their stakes, even when that can't make up for their loss, a pure order effect. Thomas Buser, a Swiss-Dutch economist, demonstrated this by paying students to participate in an arithmetic competition. A third of participants were informed correctly when they'd won, a third when they'd lost, and a third received no information at all. Men who were told they'd lost took bigger than average risks in a subsequent game, leading to earnings 20 percent lower during the remainder of the competitions after that first fatal game. For women that didn't apply, though: in fact they took less risk after losing (and in doing so incurred smaller losses).[8]

The difference (well, one of the differences) between men and women

Women take fewer risks than men after losing. Eva is an exception here, which cost her a substantial amount of money in this case. She tells herself that her competitive nature has worked out well in many situations. In various other contexts it really is advantageous to take a risk, for instance when requesting a salary rise. Why do women more often avoid risks than men, then? Of course it's completely random whether someone throws heads or tails – but what if Eva thought she was simply 'bad' at tossing coins? That very thought is disastrous. Women more often have this kind of self-fulfilling prophecy mindset: in competitive situations they're more likely than men to attribute the outcome to their own failings instead of bad luck or laziness (the attribution fly from chapter 1 has less effect on women). In response they make less effort and tend to perform worse after losing.[9]

'Lean in!' was the rallying cry of Sheryl Sandberg, former COO of Facebook, and with good reason, but why women are more reticent to take risks remains unclear. Perhaps

> different hormonal reactions to winning and losing are at the root of the difference between men and women. After gambling, the testosterone levels of winners of either sex rise more than that of losers, and testosterone leads to more risk-taking.[10] But there are also people who end up with higher blood testosterone levels in response to loss, and they go on to raise the stakes, as Eva did in the restaurant.[11]
>
> What Eva learned from this is by all means be competitive, but if you lose, think twice about raising your stakes.

Even when there's no question of winning or losing, *M.t. consequentiae* can be a matter of life and death. It all comes down to decision fatigue. This can make the moment when your case is heard by the court a determining factor in the verdict. Whether you're visiting the GP, or you've ended up in hospital or before a judge, the chance of receiving better-thought-out treatment is substantially higher if you're there earlier rather than later. At the end of the working day healthcare professionals wash their hands less frequently,[12] doctors more often prescribe antibiotics without good reason,[13] and judges become stricter in their decisions.[14] None of these are enormous effects, but to be on the safe side we personally prefer to make important decisions at the start of the day.

How your memory leaves you in the lurch

You perceive your memory as a hard drive full of stored information, but in reality you're constantly rewriting it. Your brain doesn't work the way you think it does, and that opens up opportunities for housefly effects. You can cultivate a more pleasant memory by intentionally ending your holiday on a high. Think of the last time you had flu. While the days you had fever went by in a kind of haze – because yes, they were all kind of alike – after the event all you remember of that week is a single moment. There's a good chance that you primarily remember the last part, when you were on the mend and things weren't so bad. Oh yeah, afternoon naps, daytime TV and chicken soup, happy days.

This phenomenon has been thoroughly mapped out by Daniel Kahneman. He observed that people undergoing a colonoscopy (not the loveliest of procedures, uncomfortable, scary and painful) couldn't recall clearly how long it took. How bad people found it in retrospect didn't correspond with the average discomfort or duration. It was as if people remembered snapshots; how they felt afterwards was determined by the most intense point and the final moments. He called this the **peak-end rule**.[15] Since then doctors have learned to keep all instruments still for the final minutes of a procedure. While the internal examination ends up taking longer, it feels on average less uncomfortable and leads to more positive evaluations.

The feeling that time moves faster the older you become (or the less that happens – remember the coronavirus lockdowns) has a physical cause. Psychological time consists of a series of incoming sensory information. The processing speed of those senses gradually slows as you age and the frequency of eye movements drops.[16] We also adapt our experience and expectations to the situation, and the same goes for our senses: due to desensitisation of your nose, you don't smell your own deodorant after a while. Tim particularly enjoyed a commercial that used the scary term odour blindness for this phenomenon: maybe your house stinks! It's precisely this adaptability that has a big impact on the way we remember. When the situation remains unchanged for a long time, we make fewer new memories and it feels like time goes faster.

Now you know how unreliable your memory is, you won't be

surprised to learn that our ability to predict events is not particularly precise either. You imagine something based on your memories of how you felt last time and project that onto the situation in question. Tim regularly knows for sure that he really does have enough vinyl records now, and we're sure you have your own examples. People are very bad at predicting how they'll feel and behave in a different situation. This is known as the **hot/cold empathy gap**. *Hot* here stands for a state of excitement, desire or hunger, and *cold* for the opposite, or the absence of excitement. If you've just eaten, it's easy to imagine you'll keep your hands off the savoury snacks this evening. A couple of hours later, though...

Picture this...

The more thoroughly you envision a particular situation, the better you can predict what you'll do. 'Think of something you're planning to do tomorrow (an early morning run, for instance). When you wake up in the dark, that cold outside world doesn't seem particularly inviting. So the evening before, imagine precisely how it will go. Are you sure you won't sleep through your alarm? What route will you take? What if your running buddy calls to say she's not coming, who's your back-up? More importantly, how do you feel when you get moving? Stiff and awkward at first, then finding your pace, chapped lips and the mist of your breath! By vividly picturing how you'll feel when you're there, and what could go wrong, you'll plan better and increase the chances of actually getting going.'

Doing something about it of course begins with recognising the influence of particular situations. Former professor of psychology and marketing[17] Robert Cialdini, the man who may have influenced the greatest number of people after Jesus, describes having two writers within him: a good writer and, ahem, an academic writer. His most famous book, *Persuasion*, was written in part in his university office and in part at home. At the university he wrote the opening sentence: 'My academic sub-discipline, experimental social psychology, has as its main domain the study of the social influence process.' So much for that. Once home he read the opening sentence and changed it to 'I am not afraid to admit it: I am a gullible shmuck.' The context (he alternated writing spots) had such an influence on the state of mind of this master of influence that two distinct voices were discernible in his book,* but he only noticed when he reread his work.

No time, no money, just stress

People with little to spend sometimes do strange things. They buy scratch cards and lottery tickets, save too little and borrow too much, all habits that make them poorer. You might almost think it was 'in their nature' – that, besides circumstances such as education and social environment, character traits lay at the foundation of such choices.

That's an enormous misconception. Countless studies show that temporary poverty has a negative effect on decision making – albeit also temporarily. Poverty is not the result of bad decisions, but the cause of them. It invokes a particular state of mind that attracts the *M.t. praesentiae* housefly. This was demonstrated a few years ago with farmers in India, who harvest their crops twice a year and are therefore only paid twice a year. At the end of the season the farmers scored far lower on an IQ test than just after the harvest; poverty had approximately the same impact as not

---

* As you can tell, Tim and Eva generally write at home.

sleeping the night before the test. Someone who's just been paid makes more sensible decisions than someone busy working out in their head how to make ends meet.*

Now you may not think you have much in common with farmers in India, but everyone who suddenly finds themselves short of money responds more short-sightedly. That state of mind is caused not only by lack of funds but also by lack of time. Or, in other words, the way CEOs deal with work deadlines is just as unwise as the way poor people deal with a payment deadline.

Time is money?

Of course it is. How much is an hour of your time worth? It varies from person to person; the hourly wage of a soup-serving CEO do-gooder is worth more to the foodbank than their labour, but regardless of our income, on average we have about the same amount of time per person in our lives. Analysis of 14 million taxi journeys provided by a ride-sharing service enabled researchers to study very precisely how much we're prepared to spend to get a taxi to come faster. The researchers added at random 0, 60, 150 and 240 seconds to the estimated time of arrival and looked to see whether the customer accepted the lift for a particular price. In doing so they calculated what we consider our time to be worth.

A good estimate is seriously influential: the government uses such figures, for example to calculate how much to invest in public transport and how much economic growth

---

* Tip for students: explain this to your parents, so that they lend you money *before* your exams.

Time has wings

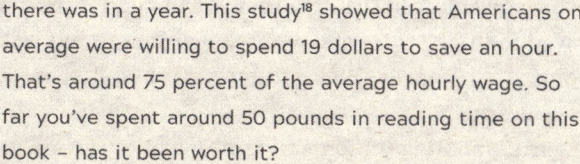

there was in a year. This study[18] showed that Americans on average were willing to spend 19 dollars to save an hour. That's around 75 percent of the average hourly wage. So far you've spent around 50 pounds in reading time on this book – has it been worth it?

In order to systematically compare deadline stress with financial stress, you need to deliberately stress people out. Behavioural scientists are creative tormentors: they invited students to play a game and gave some participants fewer turns than others. The games varied from Hangman to a version of Angry Birds, in which the player attempts to topple a pile of pigs using a catapult loaded with a bird bomb. The 'rich' were given five times as many shots. Using this trick the researchers revealed that being 'poor' undermines thinking capacity.

The poorer players spent far more time aiming than the rich, which resulted in more hits, but that's about it for the good news. The higher scores of the poor dried up when they were given the option of 'borrowing' an extra go from the next round. An extra turn cost two turns from the next round, the equivalent of 100 percent interest. Despite the high price, the poor players borrowed twelve times as often as the rich players, resulting in a significant loss. According to the researchers, that could be explained by the poor people being so focused on the current round that they lost sight of the future.

What happened when, rather than having fewer turns, people had less time to answer? In a game of 'five against five', in which a player has to give the most frequently mentioned answers to questions such as 'What would you take on a picnic?', participants were given a glimpse of questions from subsequent rounds. 'Rich' people, this time people with more time to think, performed considerably better due to that preview. The poor, under time pressure, barely noticed the tips. They even bought extra time to be allowed to think for longer about the current round, without benefiting at all from it. Lack of time therefore had the same effect as poverty.[19]

In essence, a shortage of something, be it money or time, causes the present bias fly to buzz ever louder, at the expense of things that seem less urgent. That's why stressed people make the same errors, whether they're dealing with bills or deadlines.[20]

Protection against ourselves?

Imagine your partner were to participate in the previous game, and you were in control of the rules. What would you do if your partner wanted to borrow an extra turn from the next round, knowing it has such a negative outcome?

- ☐ forbid it
- ☐ advise against it
- ☐ assign your partner to the group that doesn't have that option

To many people option 3 seems perfectly reasonable. Apply that to society. If you were a politician, would you have the courage to argue for a ban on payday loans? Providers of such easily accessible, extremely expensive, short-term loans often reason that people know what's good for them. If someone wants to borrow money, they will have thought carefully about it. But now that you know that people short of money make unwise decisions, and you want to protect your partner from them, why wouldn't you want to protect others?

You might at least want to warn people, to provide them with protection against themselves. There has been a great deal of experimentation with advice against payday loans. Two thousand websites offering such loans with exorbitant interest placed a warning, 'Beware: borrowing money costs money.'[21] What do you reckon, how much did it help?*

Time for a solution

Deadlines cause stress, and as we just observed, stress leads to bad decisions. Fortunately there's something you can do about that: deadlines can be planned well or badly. Smart timing has an immense housefly effect. People are ready to change their behaviour, for instance, in a year ending in a nine.† That's very handy if you want to advertise round-the-world trips or degree courses. Apparently there's something magical to the threshold between nine and the next ten.[22]

That magic applies to deadlines too. When a deadline goes over a particular boundary, such as the end of the month or year, people think of it as a long way off. In a study Canadian students were asked when they would begin a task. Participants for whom the deadline was next month, 'way off in the future', started the task far later than those for whom the deadline fell in the same month.

That kind of procrastination isn't exclusive to students in Toronto, the researchers realised. Indian farmers also suffered from this malady.‡ They were given the opportunity to save for their children's education. If they saved a minimum number of rupees in six months, they received a bonus. Whether they succeeded

---

* It didn't, according to a nuanced report by the Dutch financial regulator (Effectiviteit Kredietwaarschuwing (Effectiveness of credit warning), 2016).
† The fact that Eva started this book at the age of 39 is a complete coincidence, of course.
‡ Now you're thinking, why are these researchers so obsessed with Indian farmers? The reason is in part economic: Indian farmers are cheaper to enlist than Canadian students. But in part it's less cynical. Sendhil Mullainathan, one of the 2019 winners of the Nobel Prize in Economic Sciences, is the founder of the Abdul Latif Jameel Poverty Action Lab at MIT and likes to conduct useful research – such as the effect of houseflies on the very poorest people in society.

didn't depend on how much money they were prepared to spend on their children. The determining factor turned out to be whether the deadline fell before or after the end of the year. Twenty-eight percent of the people approached in June (deadline: 1 December) saved enough for the bonus, while only 4 percent of those approached in July (deadline: 1 January) managed.

What makes us knuckle down quicker when something seems closer? The closer the task comes, the more concretely we visualise the activity. The step from resolving to 'get organised' to an actual to-do list is what makes people get started on a task. In order to be able to take that step, it's therefore important not to allow any temporal boundary to intervene between now and the task. If you've resolved to do something, then start just *after* such a time threshold, as that really does seem to increase the chance of success.

Greater success with a monotonous calendar

Success depends more on getting things done than on intelligence. If you want to make something feel real, then mark the days in your calendar immediately preceding the deadline, perhaps by highlighting them in the same colour as the deadline itself. Many calendars work with two colours, for instance alternating colours for weeks, or using a different colour for the weekend and the working week. The suggestion of temporal boundaries invoked by the colour differences caused the students in the experiment to use vague platitudes for their resolutions: they would 'work on their fitness' instead of 'run five kilometres tomorrow morning'. So buy or download a calendar in a single colour; it brings unity, making deadlines look closer and inspiring you to start work sooner.

Now you'll be thinking, I'm onto this temporal fly, I can see straight through it. Sadly marketers are familiar with it too. A new mother switching laundry detergent after the arrival of a baby may not surprise you, but did you know that a new father will also more readily switch beer brand? Life events are enormous predictors of what people buy. Conversely, database marketers can use their algorithms to deduce all kinds of details from apparently innocent purchases. For instance alarm bells start ringing at credit card companies when someone suddenly makes a lot more payments in nightclubs. There's a divorce on the way, along with financial problems. Let's lower that limit! It's extra-painful when such a scoop is also made public. There's a famous example in which a man discovered that his girlfriend was pregnant from reading the supermarket discount mail. The wine had suddenly disappeared from the basket and had been replaced by certain specific vitamins... The algorithm knows how to interpret it: your 'customer journey' as a parent has begun, and there's a great deal to be earned there. (In the UK marketers have even worked out that you consider that creepy, so once in a while among your personalised offers they'll throw in a product that deviates from the norm, a whisky deal for instance. A cunning housefly that gives the illusion of privacy.)

At the other end of the spectrum, policy makers are becoming increasingly aware of life events. Imagine that new father for a moment. His name's Sander, he's just registered the birth of his child, he's responsibly switched to a single speciality beer a week and now leaves work at four to pick up his child from nursery. At home he finds his wife in bed with the neighbour. This is a serious life event – for him, but also from the perspective of government organisations: suddenly Sander is applying for a divorce, changing his mortgage and receiving maintenance payments. Due to the mental load and time pressure he may well forget to inform the tax authority that he's now deducting fewer hours for childcare. It's a minor error but he'll receive a harsh punishment.

In 2020 in the Netherlands this example was headline news in a big public scandal: lots of rules are made on the assumption that citizens systematically consider their situation and have the headspace to do so. Because this temporarily doesn't apply to people like Sander, for several years now the capacity-to-act test has applied to new regulations. Every new rule is examined for the amount of information someone has to provide, whether they have to do this proactively, and the consequence of accidentally failing to do so. Because of course it doesn't necessarily require a big life event to make people forgetful.

Conversely, the government also avails itself of the temporal fly. Ten years ago the Dutch tax service sent out blue envelopes containing a handwritten note which read, 'Could you manage this in the next ten days? Thanks. Lisa.' After receiving that note, mentioning a close, concrete deadline, the procrastinators on average submitted their tax returns five days earlier. That saved the tax service a great deal of work in follow-up phone calls. GPs, dentists and hairdressers have also discovered the power of sending reminders.

Watch your words

What can *you* do, besides sending yourself reminder mails? One solution lies in the language you use. Psychologically, the future seems more remote when you use separate words for it. You might say, 'Aaargh, it's raining again tomorrow.' 'It's raining' is the same grammatical tense as if you were talking about today. Alternatively, you could say, 'Oh dear, it's going to rain again tomorrow.' Between us and the future are the words 'going to'. In fact languages such as Dutch have no formal grammatical future tense.

Time has wings

> Which nation do you think saves more, retires richer, smokes less, has safer sex and stays slimmer: the Dutch or the Brits? That's right, it's the Dutch! On average people who keep the future distant in their language are less committed to their future selves.[23] You can even see the difference in children in the same year in school in Merano (North Italy, a bilingual region). The German-speaking pupils, with no grammatical future tense, did far better in the marshmallow test than the Italian speakers. If you want to get something done, you're better off avoiding 'will' or 'going to'.

Procrastination leads to misery

Seinfeld pointed out that for most people the end of the month sounds the same as the end of time. Ever heard of **present bias** or **hyperbolic discounting**? These are scientific terms for a phenomenon you're sure to be familiar with: to your brain, your future self is a stranger. Or perhaps even a fictitious character. You *know* you're that person, but you feel a good deal less committed to them than to your present self. This is reflected in Tim's behaviour when he saddles his elderly future self with yet another colourful tattoo. Eva encounters it when she passes on a deadline to a future Eva (*M.t. procrastinationis*). Perhaps you struggle to get yourself to save for a pension or to finally pay off a bit more of that mortgage. A small (emotional) reward in the short term can confer a large housefly effect.

Just think back to the marshmallows. An impatient person would think: I'll have that sweet now, not in five minutes. But ask that same individual: what would you prefer, one sweet in a month's time, or two sweets in a month *plus five minutes*? Then even the impatient person picks the latter option. If you place the sweet in front of them exactly a month later, the housefly wins again and the chances of the same individual waiting five minutes are slim. The earlier self has clearly done a lousy job of judging their future self – or, in any case, overestimated their future self-control.

When it comes to pleasant events, we're impatient: I want the books I've ordered to arrive today, and am happy to pay a little bit extra for it. We like to postpone awkward tasks. We'll take the glass bottles to the recycling bin and tackle the life admin tomorrow, clip the dog's nails the day after. These two traits, impatience and procrastination, go hand in hand, which is remarkable, given that, at face value, you might expect procrastinators to be more patient. Are they?

You can measure impatience, as the marshmallow test has demonstrated. The same test, not with sweets but with hard cash, was conducted among a group of students. They were invited to choose whether they took a sum of money or received the same amount plus a bit extra two weeks later. Sixty-five percent preferred to receive the money now instead of 2 percent extra in two weeks. A proportion of them didn't even change tack for 12 percent interest in two weeks. It's not entirely coincidental that the latter group, the 'I want it now' characters, were the last in their years to submit their applications.

But that wasn't the end of it. The researchers had built in a loophole to the payment. The students received their reward not as cash but as cheques (which isn't as old-fashioned in the US as it is in many other countries). That meant the researchers were able to find out when someone had actually cashed the cheque. The result was amusing: the impatient group, who decided to forego more money in order to be paid quickly, actually took longer to cash in.[24]

So procrastination isn't an isolated bad habit, but is tied to impatience. Somehow that makes sense: prompt gratification (looking at our Twitter feed right now, instant access to your money) feels

Time has wings

more important than a long-term goal (writing a book, accumulating interest). The temporal fly strikes again.

Help is at hand, though: you can pin down your future self right now. On websites such as stickK.com you can set down your goal (quitting smoking, taking up the piano) in a verifiable form and put money on it. If you procrastinate, your cash goes to a good cause (or, to make it worse for yourself, you can choose a *bad* cause). If you're patient, you can claim it back.

But watch out: don't forget to claim it right away.

Paying not to work out

What kind of people burden themselves with that sort of **commitment**? Would you do it? According to a famous article with the magnificent title 'Paying not to go to the gym' (2006),[25] there are different types of people. And of course gyms come up with membership packages for all of them.

1. The rational types: they consider how often their future self will go to the gym, select the cheapest membership package to fit and visit the gym exactly that frequently.

2. People who have some idea what their future selves will be like – and push themselves to work out by signing up for a year's membership so that they *have* to keep going.

3. The naïve types: the people who think that their future selves will go to the gym nine times in a month, and therefore sign up for 'unlimited' membership, and in practice spend 70 dollars a month on average to work out four times (when a ten-visit pass would only cost them 10 dollars a go instead of 17).

The Housefly Effect

4. The sophisticated naïve type: the person who opts for monthly membership, precisely because they're afraid of falling into category 3, but forgets to cancel every month, thus ending up even worse off than category 3.

Fortunately, there are solutions to rein in your idiocy. Just choose what you think works best (you'll find the answer after the list):

[ ] I'll get someone to pay me for going to the gym.

[ ] I'll buy the 'gym pact', designed by Harvard students who had read the article above, and pay them money if I skip my workout for a week.

[ ] I'll do some **temptation bundling** and keep my Harry Potter audio book in a locker at the gym.

The last option worked the best! Behavioural scientist Katy Milkman tested this concept, first on herself, then on a large group of students. (Her article was titled 'Holding *The Hunger Games* hostage at the gym'.) The students who paired something fun exclusively with workouts visited the gym 50 percent more frequently and were even willing to pay extra for the 'kidnapping' of their favourite book.*

---

* There's an earnings model in this, the economist in Eva thinks. Tim looks forward to the audio book of *The Housefly Effect*.

Use the fly to your advantage

In the absence of a time machine there's a good technique that can produce positive housefly effects: commitment. But you have to know how to use it.

At the core is a real problem that every employee recognises: lack of willpower. We generally don't work as hard as we think we will. Procrastination affects everyone from students to sole traders. You ought to finish something today, but a message comes in that's simply more fun – you'll get the task done tomorrow. But Instagram still exists the next day, and by then there's something else that needs finishing. If you work for a boss, procrastination has even bigger consequences. Not only are you always rushing to meet your deadlines, it might even cost you a pay rise or bonus, and it also costs your employer money.

Three economists have shown that something can be done. Procrastination by employees, in this case 124 Indian data entry workers, was influenced by when and how they were paid for their work. Even more importantly: the employees are conscious of the fact that they tend to procrastinate and quite keen to do something about it for themselves.[26]

The employees generally received 0.03 rupees per data field they had filled in (that's 0.03 pence – on average they earned about 2.25 pounds per day). During the experiment, which lasted eleven months, they were also invited to choose whether they wanted to set a target. If they did, then they received 0.03 rupees per data field only if they succeeded in filling in at least 4,000 fields per day, and the rate fell to 0.015 if they achieved fewer than 4,000. So, objectively, it was a bad choice to impose a target, but the target structure might make their lazy future selves work harder.

It turned out that the day on which the employees were paid had a huge influence on how fast they typed, with an average of 7 percent more on pay day. The effect varied substantially from person to person: some worked 20 percent harder that day, others consistently throughout the week, but the pace increased on average as pay day approached.

And yes, people were aware of their weakness. On 35 percent of days people imposed a target on themselves, to remain motivated to at least achieve that number of data fields. It sounds unwise, but it turned out that the Indian employees knew themselves well: they worked so much harder due to that target that they earned 2 percent more than their colleagues without one. It benefited their employer too.

Try this at home

If you sometimes teach a course or wish to get something done by a group, this is the method:

Step 1: ask who is planning on doing homework.

Step 2: ask them if they're sure.

Step 3: ask if they would like to **commit**. If they don't fulfil their promise, they have to pay a pound / get a point deducted.

Step 4: show them the results of last year's exam – these are always higher for the group that makes this kind of commitment, even when those who break it have a point deducted.

Step 5: ask one more time and take a photo of the show of hands.

You're guaranteed to receive more homework on time, and the students achieve higher grades![27]

So there are ways to make both employer and employee happier (or at least a bit better off), and the government, too, has ambitions in this direction. The study that made the term *nudge* famous is also about how employees establish commitments. In this case it involved far higher sums of money – and it's something you can apply yourself.

Nudge, the book in question, describes the 'Save more tomorrow' programme with which Richard Thaler made headlines. He offered employees the option to save a larger percentage towards their pension each time they received a pay rise. Note, it sounds boring, but this programme prompted 15 million people to save more than they would otherwise have done. Be sure to do this with your own savings account, because it conquers at least three housefly effects at once: you avoid the feeling of your current self 'losing out', because you still receive something of a wage increase. By asking if you want to do something in three years' time, you avoid getting bogged down in more immediate spending priorities, as you're taking the money from your future self. And finally, if you commit now, you remain on the programme unless you actively opt out. Of course you still could... but what are the chances that future self of yours will put off taking action until tomorrow?

Fly swatter at the ready!

In this chapter you've discovered how many housefly effects are based on timing and the order in which things happen. You've probably retained some great scientific terms too. The next time you start work too late, you can say: sorry, I was massively delayed by **hyperbolic discounting**! And from now on you're sure to avoid saving an annoying chore until the last day of a lovely holiday, as the **peak-end rule** tells us that'll ruin your entire memory of it.

Luckily, there's even more you can do to combat order effects, timing techniques and procrastination, while still having things your own way. The fly swatters from this chapter fall into two categories: changing something in the outside world or changing the way you view the future.

In the first category are techniques like those used by the data entry workers: making a **commitment**. The gym members did the same: they paired something pleasant (the audio book) inextricably with something useful (the gym). The government constructed a whole new option, an automatically increasing contribution. And the icing on the cake is building in 'pitfalls' for your future self, such as an app which shuts Twitter down after four minutes. (Eva doesn't need an app; her child is quite capable of that.)

Less drastic interventions which also very effectively combat temporal houseflies are aimed at changes in your perception of the situation, rather than changes to the outside world. Start by choosing the right moment for your resolution. If you're hungry, don't go shopping; if you're stressed, don't place any faith in your willpower. A 'fresh' moment works better: a new month, a new computer, a new partner.

The more specifically you picture your goal in the future, the more achievable it becomes. The more vivid the memory, the more willing you are to do something to repeat it – it feels closer... Remember how badly your memory functions (like we mentioned a few pages back? Never mind). That's why it works very well when you imagine the future benefit in as much detail as possible, encompassing all your senses.* Don't forget to think through what might come between you and your resolutions. The technical term is **implementation intentions**.

How do you make a goal concrete? Say, you've been meaning to cancel your underutilised gym membership since before the pandemic.

---

* Does this put you in mind of *The Secret*? You'll read any pseudoscientific self-help trash going, won't you?

Time has wings

1. Write an email to yourself with the advantages – make it specific (the monthly sum you'll save).

2. Think what you can do about this and when (log into the website tonight).

3. Think what might get in the way (not being able to find your password).

4. Write down what you'll do if that happens (request a password reset).

5. Pro tip: avoid the future tense!*

Many of these solutions mainly work well when they're combined with social pressure. Commitments work when they're public. Remember Odysseus tying himself to the mast to resist the temptation of the Sirens: he deafened his sailors to his pleas by blocking their ears with wax. That may be taking things a little far, but of course you can also ask your friends to block your phone number if you want to study all evening.

You can use order effects for your own benefit, or that of your business, as well. Some café loyalty schemes offer you every tenth drink free and often have the first stamp preprinted on the card. Do the same with your future plans: make sure you've already cycled to work a couple of times, because breaking a streak is a shame and feels like a loss. So what are you waiting for? Quick, turn over and keep your reading streak going with chapter 6.

---

* 'On Monday I'm cancelling my gym membership,' rather than 'I'm going to cancel my gym membership.'

> The attraction fly is irresistible.

Musca attractionis

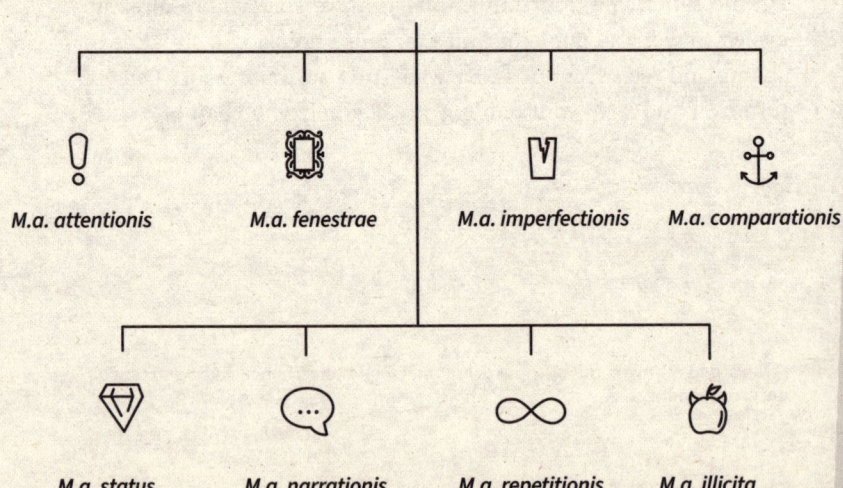

M.a. attentionis *M.a. fenestrae* *M.a. imperfectionis* *M.a. comparationis*

M.a. status *M.a. narrationis* *M.a. repetitionis* *M.a. illicita*

Chapter 6

The force of attraction

***Musca attractionis* or 'attraction fly'**

Subspecies: *M.a. attentionis* (attention), *M.a. fenestrae* (framing), *M.a. imperfectionis* (imperfection), *M.a. comparationis* (comparison), *M.a. status*, *M.a. narrationis* (narrative), *M.a. repetitionis* (repetition), *M.a. illicita* (illicit).

A common fly that appears in a wide variety of settings, from luxury goods to time-wasting apps and even apples, especially when they're compared with oranges. Seemingly domesticated and well-trained by advertisers, spin doctors and pickup artists, *Musca attractionis* is also known as the 'chameleon fly', as it comes in many different guises. While possibly the most conspicuous housefly species, the havoc it can wreak is often underestimated.

Have you seen the film classic *Magnolia*? It stars Tom Cruise as a motivational speaker who teaches roomfuls of lonely, insecure men how to attract women. For a hefty fee, of course. His character is creepy, offensive, extremely misogynistic and, yes, true to life. Because they exist, these 'PUAs', or pickup artists, who lead well-attended seminars on how to trick a woman into giving you her phone number. The curriculum is a curious mixture of the psychology, chicanery, science and clichés that we've come to associate with Andrew Tate. The first big question that springs to mind – after 'is this legitimate?' and 'how scary is this?' – is, of course: does it actually work? Is it just a clever con or is attraction something that can be taught? However much we like to unmask cunning scams, these courses do appear to have some effect. That's partly down to the specific target audience, of course. Someone who's never had the guts to ask someone out prior to one of these pep talks is bound to derive at least some benefit from them.

Aside from that, the techniques that are taught also appear to be paying dividends. How so? That's exactly what journalist Neil Strauss asked himself. In his book *The Game*[1] he describes delving into this community and getting caught up in it, to the extent that he ends up becoming the ultimate dodgy guy who teaches young men how to seduce 'the ladies'.* The men involved borrow

---

* Parents, we urge you to buy a copy for your daughters.

techniques from illusionists and mediums and hand out cheap jewellery with fibs like 'this used to belong to my late mother'.

We wouldn't want to withhold their most striking trick from you. Strauss and his pupils frequent the LA clubs with dryer lint in their back pockets. When they spot a nice woman, they pretend to pick a sizable bit of fluff off her back. Strauss sums up nicely why that's so effective: it leaves the woman momentarily flustered and maybe even embarrassed about walking around with it all evening. In other words, the pickup artist has brought her down a peg, has initiated physical contact and has even done something kind. But you, the reader, will have cottoned on to what's really happening here: these disciples of *The Game* have trained a whole bunch of houseflies with one thing in common: they make something or someone attractive.

The *Musca attractionis* family features flies that make you feel that something or someone is a good match for you, as well as flies that evoke a sense of pride, luxury and status that, strictly speaking, has nothing to do with the thing itself. Houseflies that encourage you to compare something with a far less attractive counterpart; that get you to look at it through a different lens; that make you feel that something is familiar, or else surprising and interesting. And last but not least: flies that secretly seduce you into paying attention to something.

Grabbing attention, hacking attention

Becoming attractive starts with receiving attention, and that's true for our dodgy pickup artists as much as anything. The simple fact that something has your attention has an effect on your opinion of it: the **focusing illusion**. Subconsciously, you're reasoning: I noticed this; my clever brain actually picked out this thing or this person.* Surely that must make it worthwhile? This sensation is

---

* Hey, it's our old friend self-overestimation again!

most acute in an environment designed to engender 'attention mode'. For instance, when you walk into a room in a museum, you automatically slow down and lower your voice in response to the respectful silence and echoey acoustics. The white walls show the artworks to their best advantage. Your eyes follow the beam of a single spotlight and alight on a bin bag that's been carefully placed against the wall. Now, for the first time, you become aware of the unique texture of this mundane object: at once smooth and rough. The colour, not simply black but a deep anthracite, is more beautiful than you ever realised. It's almost moving. Your thoughts go out to all the beauty in everyday life, which is so often overlooked, and your hand reaches for your mobile, because this profound idea must be tweeted, alongside a photo of this gorgeous piece of installation art. And then someone behind you barks: 'What are you doing in the cleaning cupboard?'

That power of attention is also harnessed when you carefully sip a glass of wine in a restaurant. Such a complexity of flavours and aromas! And when you're totally focused on a film in the cinema. That very same film can be disappointing as you watch it again at home on your sofa, chatting to your partner, with your phone in hand. It's what many feel while meditating: attention changes your experience. That means it influences what you do, choose or buy. What holds your attention seems more interesting, more important, and the more intently we look at something, the more we see (and the more beauty we see). The company that can direct your focus to its product, service, app or gadget takes an immediate 5-0 lead. It's no wonder then that the battle for our attention is so intense. But what is surprising is how often it's won by deploying seemingly insignificant little flies.

Does the name Party Cannon ring a bell? There's every chance it does, as the British death metal band has gone viral no fewer than three times. With their deafening music? Their doom-laden lyrics? No, with their logo. In their scene, the visuals are all pretty similar: horror-style, jagged black-and-white letters, like ominous cracks in stone. Nearly all anyway, as Party Cannon have bucked the trend and have opted for a cheerful, multicoloured balloon-like font that looks more at home in a toy shop. It makes them stand out from other bands on festival posters. It's one hell of a housefly, that typeface. The headbangers managed to become the talk of the town without changing a single note of their music. It wasn't the colourful logo in and of itself; if it adorned children's toys, nobody would bat an eyelid. The thing itself isn't attention-grabbing, but the contrast with its surroundings is. Wear a tuxedo to a premiere and you blend in with the crowd. But, having misread a party invitation's 'smart-casual' dress code, one of Tim's colleagues was the only one to wear a tux and ended up being the centre of attention all night.

How come? As mentioned earlier, your brain has to conserve energy, so it scans the environment for a pattern. There's no need to be wasteful and focus on anything that fits the mould: it's predictable, normal. Something that deviates does require attention, though: it could be dangerous – or attractive. Think about it: in a new house you notice every little noise. But you soon learn which creaks and groans are normal and you stop hearing them. Once your brain recognises the pattern you're only startled by sounds that deviate from this. Not unlike the man who was jolted awake and cried out, 'What was that?!' when for once the train didn't thunder past his house at three in the morning.

The phenomenon of distinctive things standing out is named after the scientist who did a great deal of research into it during the twentieth century: the **Von Restorff effect**.* Few advertising execs will be familiar with that term, but they'll certainly be aware of the effect itself. That's why they're always trying to make *their* brand feel different, by using spectacular visuals or unique

---

* Related to the availability bias from chapter 2.

The Housefly Effect

guarantees, by turning a business model on its head or simply by having an ad that's so annoying that you can't ignore it.

But this housefly is also baked into products themselves. If you've ever seen a Swapfiets bicycle, you'll have noticed its distinctive blue front tyre, which means this little fly has got a hold of you. It's not as if these rental bikes have flooded the market, they're just more conspicuous than the ones with regular black tyres. Apple achieved something similar with the white earbuds that came with the first iPods. Since all other earphones were black at the time, the sight of white buds would have you thinking: ah, another person with an iPod. Apple's astute TV commercials featured dancing black silhouettes with brilliantly white earbuds. Years later, when nearly all earbuds were white, Apple followed up with its distinctive AirPod design. All of a sudden, everybody seemed to be wearing these weird white 'earrings'. A coincidence? Of course not. Apple knows its houseflies.

And it's not alone. Advertisers, the media, app developers, governments: in the battle for your attention, they pull out all the stops. Flashing buttons, beeping notifications and impossible-to-ignore red numbers on your phone. Colourful digital billboards* in the street and a big bag of fries on the façade of the chip shop. On the radio, the ads seem to get louder and louder and if that doesn't work the makers throw in sound effects.† But while such blatant begging for your attention may be annoying, the opposite could well be worse. Companies 'hack' your attention with all kinds of more subtle houseflies. Remember, back in the day, when a lottery or charity would send out mass mailings and you could feel there was something inside the envelope? A sticker, pen or

---

* Tim loves them, which is why he got married in Las Vegas. His wife must be amazing.
† Some free advice for advertisers: don't use sirens, because listeners will switch off the radio to check where they're coming from. Houseflies don't always fly in their intended direction.

coin, it was never anything big, but it did pique your interest. The modern variant of this is the company that pictures a realistic-looking hair on its mobile banner ad. When you try to brush it off your screen, you swipe straight to the web shop. Those devious digital tricks are known as dark or deceptive patterns. We used them in the advertising for this book, albeit ironically, by making it look as if a little fly had landed on our banners.

Kindness and all that jazz

Let's take another look at those dodgy pickup artists. These guys have lots of tricks up their sleeve to catch your attention: dance moves, sleight of hand, you name it. But, in our dryer lint example, they opted for something kind.* That's pretty remarkable when you consider that American reality TV contestants tend to live by the motto: 'I didn't come here to make friends.' Whether it's a new business venture, becoming the next top model or cooking the tastiest steak, if it's success you're after, you need to be tough as nails. It explains the popularity of workshops that teach you how to stop being a people-pleaser and of self-help books about putting yourself first. Being nice gets you nowhere, and it's lonely at the top, right? No, wrong. Some clichés contain a grain of truth, but these are ready for the scrapheap. Research suggests that people who are selfish at work aren't actually more successful. Any short-term gain is soon cancelled out by a lack of teamworking skills. The opposite *is* true, though. People who are perceived to be more sympathetic are often better at winning over their colleagues. It's probably why the American classic *How to Win Friends and Influence People* is still relevant.[2]

Relatable but, come to think of it, also a bit weird. Surely, as an

---

* They make an exception for women they'd score a nine or ten. The coaches reckon that these beauties are so used to flattery that they're fascinated by you if you show a lack of interest or act like a prick.

The Housefly Effect

intelligent person you can see past a smile, however charming it may be. Who cares whether or not you like the messenger? It shouldn't have an impact on the content of the message. But apparently it does. Empathy, the feeling that you click, have a bond: it's a big fat housefly. To quote the godfather of influence, Cialdini: 'People say "yes" to those within the boundaries of we.' It explains why Tupperware parties did so well for so long; they drew on existing family and friendship ties. But in the absence of those, there are plenty of other methods of creating a sense of connection. While the pickup artists tend to go down the creepy route, there are more subtle ways too.

When Tim joined a big, hectic advertising agency in Amsterdam, he placed a few of his favourite jazz CDs on the edge of his desk. It led to some nice chats with fellow music freaks and before long he'd met quite a few of his colleagues. And then there's the usual round of introductions at the start of a meeting. Many dread this ritual: what to say or not say? Every so often, someone will suggest skipping these intros altogether 'because of time constraints'. But then you'd miss out on the chance to build relationships of trust, and with it the opportunity to speed up the collaborative process (and future meetings). By getting to know each other better, people learn what they have in common, and that's good for teamwork. So go ahead with that round of introductions and listen carefully. Identify similarities when it's your turn.* Mention that you used to work at the same company, attended the same university, both have a young child or have both read *The Housefly Effect* – it all creates a bond.

It's why dating sites often exaggerate how much you and another singleton have in common.† Similarities are houseflies.

---

* Tip: introduce yourself as late as possible. Like you, the others are preparing mentally for their turn and will be more attentive to you once they've had their say. It's known as the next-in-line effect.
† *Married at First Sight* is the ultimate example. Tim is convinced that the mere

The force of attraction

Experiments have shown that people are more likely to respond favourably to you when you're dressed in the same style, use the same language register or share a birthday.[3] Similar-sounding names have that effect too. Your potential client is called Marco and your colleague Marc? Ask the latter to send out that quote. Why not?!

Einstein was wrong

'Insanity is doing the same thing over and over again and expecting different results.' The quote is often attributed to Albert Einstein, but whoever said it was wrong. Repetition actually has a ferocious housefly effect, at least it does when it comes to behaviour. Show somebody a commercial and the effect will be negligible. But after seven, eight, nine times, it will start to influence the viewer's choices. Repetition can make the exact same thing far more attractive. Strange as this may sound, it makes sense too. To secure your survival, your brain must identify things that are known to you, that are safe and familiar. Once you've seen something multiple times and you're still alive, you know it won't eat you. This state of affairs, when your brain recognises something and easily knows what to do, is called *processing fluency*. You could say that a particular neural pathway is starting to become engrained. That ease feels good. But watch out! Your conscious, thinking self has very little say over who or what triggers such feelings. A harmless example is this year's big summer hit; at first it bores you to tears, but over time you grow to like it. Or the regret over a retail chain disappearing from the high street even though you never bought

---

fact that you're prepared to go on this type of show means that you already have a lot in common and this will boost your chances of success. It reminds us of those silly flyers in which Mr Quack, Highly Gifted Medium, promises to sort out your sore neck, sex life and pension shortfall. The charlatans behind these cards write them so as to attract only the most gullible, desperate people, while the rest shake their heads and pass. Not quite so stupid then, those ads.

anything in its shops. Eva and Tim both live in Amsterdam and are often amazed by the 'rescue campaigns' mounted by fellow citizens. A decrepit building, a spot of graffiti, a broken bench, even a filthy public urinal – try to remove it and, before you know it, a committee has formed to save this unique bit of urban streetscape. Having seen it so often, the locals have grown to love it. It's like a mild case of Stockholm syndrome, the condition in which hostages develop feelings for their captors.

Revealed: the SHOCKING truth about fake news!

Information becomes more credible the more you see it. On social media, especially, that's a self-reinforcing cycle. Since Trump's election in 2016, platforms have tried everything in their power to guard against fake news, deploying new strategies every day.

What do you think would be most effective in combatting the spread of disinformation?

[ ] adding the source of the news

[ ] including a warning with articles that have been debunked by fact checkers

[ ] issuing a general warning: 'Beware fake news!'

[ ] promoting posts from sources that have been labelled 'trustworthy' by users

[ ] asking people to stop and think before they share something

[ ] inviting people to assess random posts for accuracy

The force of attraction

> The correct answer is: the final three options. After extensive testing on Facebook and X (formerly Twitter), it was found that options 1, 2 and 3 made little difference to the credibility and spread of fake news. The latter three did work. It goes to show that measures that, intuitively, feel useful aren't always effective.[4]
>
> How many did you get right?

Social psychologist Robert Zajonc carried out comprehensive research into this and labelled it the **mere-exposure** effect. The simple fact that you're exposed to something triggers warm feelings. Zajonc tested it by placing meaningless Chinese characters on a poster, displaying them and asking students to rate their meaning on a good–bad scale. He did this over the course of several weeks. And guess what? The more the participants saw of the symbols, the more positive their associations became. Zajonc followed this up with other versions of the experiment, some of which included images, and these too became more beautiful in the eyes of students after increased exposure. An innocuous phenomenon? You know those politicians who are always making headlines with provocative statements? Journalists no doubt believe they're doing the right thing by giving airtime to their dodgy claims. But what happens when you keep seeing that same ugly mug in the news, day in day out? After a while, he or she is still a villain, but more specifically 'your' villain. Your emotions have changed by the mere frequency of seeing that face. And when enough people have the same experience, it's going to be reflected in the election results. Talk about something small with huge repercussions...

The Housefly Effect

The devil you know

That fondness for 'your villain' can develop even when you never actually see him or her. Eva did an experiment once to test the effect. Participants were invited to play a trust exercise in which they got to invest real money (a few euros) in an opponent. Eva doubled the money and gave it to the other player who could then – voluntarily – return some of it to the original investor. Of course there were people who did so, just as there were some who kept everything to themselves. After the end of round one, participants were asked to choose who they'd rather play with: those who'd ripped them off, or someone who'd fleeced another player. You've guessed it: people preferred to play a second game with the devil they knew, even when they'd never laid eyes on him or her.

Try this at home

It goes without saying that you can use this to your advantage. Are you struggling to convince your team of the merits of your new logo design? 'Accidentally' leave the print-out on the noticeboard that they walk past every day. You bet that after a month they'll say, On second thoughts, it's pretty strong actually.'

The familiar surprise

But is there a point when something becomes *too* familiar? Yes, and when that happens we simply no longer see it. This is known as **inattentional blindness**. It's probably the cause of quite a few relationship problems and is certainly behind a great many road accidents, which often occur on habitual daily routes. The solution? A soupçon of surprise. The sight of something out of the ordinary will put you on the alert and inject a bit of tension or excitement. Combine it with that wonderful feeling of familiarity and you've got a winning formula on your hands: give people what they know and want, but in a way that's new to them. It's a rock-solid marketing strategy: want to sell something familiar? Make it feel like new. Want to sell something new? Make it feel familiar. Why do you think Apple products picture a floppy disk on their save button, use a bin as the delete icon and make a document look like a virtual sheet of A4 paper? Steve Jobs referred to this as *skeuomorphism*: wrapping something new in a well-known form.

That's why we're astonished that lots of communication experts are critical of The Vegetarian Butcher and its 'meaty' product names like *Auf Wieder Schnitzel*. Anyone with a nodding acquaintance with houseflies knows that those monikers are absolutely spot on. Perhaps that's why the farming industry called for a ban on terms such as soy 'sausage' and veggie 'burger', claiming they're confusing for consumers. The European Parliament, however, voted against restrictions and has likewise declined to outlaw descriptors such as 'buttery' and 'creamy' for plant-based dairy alternatives.*

A familiar surprise – now that's effective. You can use this insight to your advantage to select the best ideas after a brainstorming session. On a whiteboard, draw a horizontal line and divide it into four sections. Then, from left to right, jot down 'annoying', 'familiar', 'surprising' and 'confusing'. Place all your ideas on that line. Where on this spectrum would you put recent TV successes and hit songs? Probably somewhere halfway between familiar and surprising. Once something becomes *too* well-known and *too* predictable, boredom can strike. But if the element of surprise begins to dominate, you can end up confused. The sweet spot is right in the middle. It's where you'll find the best ideas.† So hopefully you'll learn a few new things from this book, but if we touch on ideas you've come across before, then that's obviously no coincidence.

There's something not quite right about perfection

There's a healthy debate in the media about the effect on our self-image of 'perfect' models. Interestingly enough, adman Tim usually seeks out models who aren't completely flawless. A perfect supermodel might be, erm, perfect for brands that sell dreams – expensive perfumes spring to mind – but if you were to place one in a supermarket commercial, which is all about real life, the effect would be counterproductive. In that case, the perfection would provoke irritation rather than adoration. Is that because

---

* That's a relief, because companies are often pretty creative in this category. Tim worked on the launch of a non-dairy milk froth and loves product names such as I Can't Believe It's Not Butter!, What, Not Butter! and Could It Be Butter?
† Directors like David Lynch and Christopher Nolan are in a category all of their own, as they tend to be reassuringly confusing for their fans.

The force of attraction

people are mean-spirited and jealous? Maybe. But there's another way of looking at it. Life teaches us that nothing is perfect. So if something or someone seems too good to be true, we become suspicious. Where's the catch? A tiny flaw can be a huge fly.

When you spot an imperfection, you lower your guard. In a famous experiment[5] two groups of participants are shown a video of someone expertly answering questions about physics. The first group sees a short version, the second gets to watch the same film, except that at the end the clever speaker spills his coffee. It may not come as a surprise that the second group felt more sympathetic towards the authority, precisely because of this gaffe, or **pratfall**. And remarkably, they also had more respect for him. This may sound strange, but it's something we also see in online stores. Products or holiday destinations peak at an average of 4.7 stars. Any more than that and it all sounds *too* perfect and therefore less credible.

We're not telling you to deliberately fall over at the end of every presentation at work, but acknowledging mistakes boosts your credibility. So go for it! But be careful. This housefly is particularly successful when we already think highly of somebody, and the blunder doesn't detract from his or her expertise. A cabinet minister who doesn't have the correct figures at his or her fingertips during a debate loses the respect of voters and colleagues. But a politician who momentarily slips out of his or her role on television is both fun and human. That person becomes more endearing, and perhaps you're just that little bit more likely to vote for him or her.

Spin and buzz

Speaking of politicians: one housefly they all love is **framing**. Now you might say: Yuck! Isn't that something that creepy spin doctors do to put one over on voters? Sure. But we bet you've been guilty of it yourself in the past week. Framing is nothing other than deciding what lens to look through. Humans have the ability to view things from different angles – but not at the same time. This is doubly true for children: show a child a tumbler of lemonade and then pour it into a highball glass. Young ones struggle to wrap their heads around the fact that both contain the same amount of liquid, so the child will be happier with the same quantity in the taller, narrower glass. We saw something similar in the scenario with the two plates of food. That's the power of framing for you, and we never quite outgrow the effect it has on our decision making.

Take the state. Does the public sector serve the general interest, or is it a bureaucracy riddled with red tape? And how about the corporate sector: hard-working entrepreneurs or industrial behemoths? It seems as if we have two distinct interpretations of these concepts in our heads, which can be 'activated' with just a few words. *The Housefly Effect*: a fun read full of useful tips or a handbook for ruthless manipulation? Have a look at the back cover to see how we frame it. We're not alone in thinking about these matters. Framing is unavoidable and everywhere. Let's start in the supermarket dairy aisle. Would you like a yoghurt that's 95 percent fat-free? Or do you prefer one that contains 5 percent fat? While they contain the same number of calories, they have a different effect on your behaviour. A noticeably higher percentage of health-conscious individuals choose the former, while it's thought they experience a fuller flavour when eating the second option.[6]

Now you may be thinking: yoghurt, what are you on about? Of course people don't care about something as trivial as that. Fair enough, but what about the next experiment?

DIY experiment

In 1981, long before the Covid pandemic, Kahneman[7] presented a group of students with the following dilemma:

The force of attraction

'An Asian epidemic is expected to cause the deaths of 600 people. Thankfully, there are remedies. Which one do you choose?'

- Programme A, which will save the lives of 200 people;
- Programme B, which gives ⅓ probability that 600 people can be spared, but ⅔ probability that nobody survives.

Pause your deliberations for a moment and find a second subject! Ask a fellow train passenger, your mother-in-law or someone in the neighbouring toilet cubicle to read the text box below and answer this question.

'An Asian epidemic is expected to cause the deaths of 600 people. Thankfully, there are remedies. Which one do you choose?'

- Programme C, which will lead to the deaths of 400 people;
- Programme D, which gives ⅓ probability of no fatalities, and ⅔ probability of 600 people dying.

What happened? You probably opted for programme A (as did 72 percent of the original cohort). Your second test subject is likely to have chosen option D, as did 78 percent in Kahneman's experiment. But let's take a closer look. Options A and C are exact equivalents! The only difference is that

The Housefly Effect

> A has been framed in positive terms, mentioning the total number of people saved instead of those dying. Options B and D are identical too, except now you're inclined to accept the risk in a last-ditch effort to save at least some people.

Framing has a huge impact, and not just on paper. The ability to recognise this housefly can be a matter of life and death. Literally. Doctors who leave treatment choices up to their patients know how important positive or negative framing (survival versus mortality) can be. What's more, they're susceptible to it themselves. It's no wonder then that we see so much of it in political wording. The US Republicans refer to their anti-abortion stance as pro-life – as if anyone could be against life. A tax on inheritance is, in their words, a death tax. Washington, built on marshland, is The Swamp, muddy, dirty and dangerous. And their party? The Grand Old Party. Even their opponents refer to it as the GOP! Trump's nadir came when he described Covid-19 as the 'Invisible China Virus'. But George W. Bush remains unbeatable, framing the armed response to a military invasion along the lines of 'I think we are welcomed. But it was not a peaceful welcome.'[8] While we're on the subject, it's interesting to note that the greatest minds in this field nearly all have Democratic leanings,* whereas the GOP, sorry, the Republicans, are best at putting the theory into practice. Perhaps wily framing is more at home with casino bosses like Trump than it is with idealists?†

---

* Such as Cass Sunstein, the author of *Nudge*, who has worked as an adviser to Obama and Biden.
† In the Netherlands, the left-leaning parties are no laggards either, with winners such as 'mansion subsidy' (the term used by socialist party SP for home mortgage interest deduction) and the 'Prince Bernhard tax' on slum landlords coined by labour party PvdA (Prince Bernhard, a cousin of the Dutch king, has a big property portfolio). But nobody, on either the left or right, is a patch on populist Geert Wilders' frames-per-minute record.

The force of attraction

Either way, ignoring the insights of behavioural science can have huge repercussions in the political arena. You have an immediate lead over your opponent when they adopt your framing and talk at length about why something *isn't* a ticking time bomb or a pernicious plague. The pro-Brexit camp made brazen use of this when it sent a big bus around the country with the UK's weekly contribution to Europe printed on its side. The figure was untrue, because it was far too high. So obviously the remainers sought to correct this in the media. They'd caught the Brexiteers lying! It wasn't 350 million pounds, but 'only' 248 million! And soon the debate in the media and among the public moved away from all the positive reasons for staying in the EU, such as peace, the economy, travel and study, and onto the amount of money that went into European coffers. That was precisely what the Leavers were after. The frame as a political mousetrap.

How do you effectively frame a discussion without making it too obvious? Aside from printing incorrect figures on buses, a commonly used method is asking questions. Tell people what the question is, and they'll automatically answer it in their heads. John F. Kennedy did it in his most famous speech: 'Ask not what your country can do for you, ask what you can do for your country.' Few people at the time responded by saying, 'Forget it, John, I'll decide what to ask myself.' That's remarkable when you think about it. But even if that was your response, and you believe you're using your critical faculties, you do still accept that this is the right question to ponder. A well-known brand of shampoo does something similar with its slogan 'because I'm worth it'. The underlying question is '*Am* I worth it?' Of course I'm worthy of that stupid shampoo of yours. Duh! But the question you're *not* asking is whether this shampoo is worth more money than the rival brand. The emphasis has shifted from the shampoo to you. You're being framed as we speak.

In politics, framing is also often done through figures of speech. Young refugees are referred to as a 'tsunami of testosterone bombs', benefits become a safety net or even a hammock, an industry is the country's engine or the driving force of society. Vendors also use such metaphors in abundance: the model you're looking at is the Rolls-Royce among inkjet printers. That sounds quite promising, but strictly speaking no firm pledges have been made. How are you going to prove that that printer is more like a Kia Picanto? The opportunities for framing by metaphor are unlimited, as much of our language is figurative in nature. Things don't literally go pear-shaped, and you're not really a million miles away or in the doldrums. And we never expect the ground to actually swallow us up. But we do talk like this. And clever framers know it.

Try this at home

Think about the metaphors you use at work and the frames they imply. Why not have a look at a thesaurus or a synonym website to see what words have similar meanings. 'Fight' is listed alongside 'do battle', 'come to blows' and 'fracas', while 'score' is linked to 'winning' and 'success'. So choose words that evoke the right associations.

If you were giving a presentation you could say: 'Go on, fire away. My team will defend itself.' But what sort of frame does this metaphor evoke? War. Enemies pitted against each other, with only one side capable of winning this fight to the death. Is that really how you want to frame the layout of the annual report? Why not try a music metaphor: 'We think this idea is a hit but we won't know for sure until we hear applause.'

Spin doctors can also work with categories, as our minds like to pigeonhole things. The label we give something has a huge impact on its perceived attractiveness. Having cake for breakfast felt decadent until we learned it was called a muffin. Cup a Soup was

The force of attraction

downright disgusting when we thought of it as a soup, but as a savoury alternative to yet another coffee, at a moment when you really need a pick-me-up: not bad at all. Behaviour can be reframed in the same way. The Mates for Life road safety campaign, which urges people to stop their mates from drink-driving, turns a potentially boring, non-drinker into a hero for getting his or her friends home safely. When public health officials called for a reduction in portion sizes in the US, the word used wasn't small – which wouldn't have gone down well in a nation where everything is supersized. No, these portions became fun-sized, and 'all you can eat' became 'all you care to enjoy'. The fishing industry is only too aware of the immense housefly effect of naming. Back in 1977 fishmonger Lee Lantz wanted to start selling a tasty and unpopular species in the US. There was just one problem: the enormous creature not only looked monstrous, but it also went by the unappetising moniker of Patagonian Toothfish. Lantz rechristened it Chilean sea bass, which has a nice ring to it and sits right in the centre of the familiar-surprising spectrum we talked about earlier. The fish became so popular under this name that measures against overfishing had to be brought in. Post-Brexit, British fishers decided to tap into a similar framing vein. They suddenly found themselves with a glut of species that were previously only sold to European countries, so in an effort to conquer the domestic market they took the creepily named spider crab, among others, and renamed it the Cornish king crab.* Framing by naming!

Yes, I agree to read this text box and enrich my knowledge with an interesting factoid!

Choices also lend themselves well to framing. Tim once worked for a big distance learning institution, which used to ask its prospective students to cut out, fill in and return

---

* It's not an endangered species yet, but give it time.

a form the old-fashioned way. One of the options they were asked to tick was always some kind of variation on: 'No, don't sign me up, I'm going to pass on this amazing offer and miss out on a wonderful future!' We can hear you say: what idiot clips a coupon out of a newspaper just to say that he doesn't want to enrol? You're right, nobody did. It was a textbook example of an *enhanced active choice*, a form of framing in which the options are formulated so as to steer the response. If you're an online shopper you'll know exactly what we mean.

[ ] Yes, of course I'd like to lock in the best possible price.

[ ] No, thanks, I'll keep flushing my hard-earned cash down the drain!

Obvious? Yep. Effective? You bet. That's why we're all doing it. And that includes you at home when, for instance, you present your loved one with these alternatives:

[ ] Are you ready?

[ ] Will you be much longer? If so, there's no point in going because we'll be too late to enjoy the festival.

We're all spin doctors. Our advice? Enjoy, but frame in moderation. And whatever you do, don't frame accidentally. This housefly can come back and bite you on the arse.

I experience perfection – when I see the housefly effect in action

Sometimes advertising takes inspiration from science. And sometimes scientists discover something that advertisers already knew. The latter is true for the **rhyme-as-reason effect**, or the **Keats heuristic**: the better a statement sounds, the more likely people are to believe it. As the expression goes, 'If it rhymes, it chimes.' The idea that the same content is more plausible when it rhymes was confirmed by the wittily titled study 'Birds of a Feather Flock Conjointly (?)'.[9] As we know, the proverb is meant to finish on 'together'. Other classics include 'red sky at night, shepherd's delight', 'when the cat's away the mice will play' and 'shop till you drop'.

So the ad makers knew full well what they were doing when they created the rhyming commercials of old ('Gillette, the best a man can get!').

Compared to what?

Among all the fine dining dishes on Daniel Bouloud's menu in New York, you'll find a hamburger. Priced at 100 dollars. Would you order it? Or do you reckon it's a bit pricey for a burger? No doubt the top chef's creation, containing Kobe beef and truffle, is tastier than a McDonald's. But for that kind of money you could order 80 at the fast-food chain! And what to make of 666 Burger, also in NYC? The food truck offers the so-called 'Douche Burger'. You're expected to eat it standing in the street, but it also contains Kobe beef and truffle as well as foie gras, caviar and lobster. And

The Housefly Effect

– a nice touch – it's wrapped in gold leaf. Official slogan: 'It may not taste good, but it will make you feel rich as f–k. Douche'. Price: 666 dollars. Would you buy one? We think we'll pop down to Maccy D's instead.

But something interesting has happened here. Thinking back to Bouloud's burger, don't you agree that it's fairly reasonably priced? Admittedly, 100 dollars is no joke. But think about what you get for that price. You even get to eat it seated at a table in a fine establishment. All that for less than a sixth of the extortionate Douche Burger! What peculiar housefly effect is at work here, easing our sense of indignation over that first burger?

Both chefs know full well what's at play: it's ***anchoring***, or the **reference effect**. People are very poor at judging things on their own merit. At the end of the day, what's cheap and what's expensive? That's why we tend to assess things, and especially figures (such as prices), by comparison. Can you pick up a packed suitcase and determine exactly how much it weighs? But if you lift first one and then another, you'll know which is heavier. The reference you're given, the anchor point, has a similarly potent housefly effect. If your jaw drops at the idea of a 666-dollar burger (anchor), a 100-dollar alternative will feel reasonably priced. It's no secret that the priciest wine on the menu is mainly there to encourage diners to choose the second most expensive option – often, the costlier one isn't even available. An Italian restaurant in London casts an even heavier anchor by having a Vespa scooter on the menu alongside the pizzas and pastas. It's yours for just under 3,000 pounds.

The force of attraction

DIY experiment

Turn to a random page in this book. Jot down the page number [...]

Take a look at this bottle of wine.

How much would you be willing to pay for it?

[£ ...,...]*

Now you may be thinking: Vespas and pizzas, that's comparing apples and oranges. Yet even a totally unrelated anchor point has an impact. For example, test subjects in a US study who'd just filled in a 'high' zip code gave more money to charity than those with a 'low' one.[10] And speaking of good causes: let's consider suggested donations. What do you think yielded higher amounts in an experiment?

I wish to donate (please select):
50   30   20   10

I wish to donate (please select):
10   20   30   50

Exactly, start with the higher figure and the average amount selected will go up.

---

* Did you write down a page number under 60? There's a fair chance you were prepared to pay less than 10 pounds for the wine. If you had a page number over 100, you probably thought it was worth more.

These so-called giving ladders are the object of careful analysis. The reverse order (low-high) can result in more donors, as the threshold for contributing is perceived to be lower. Likewise, the difference between the amounts has an influence on what people end up donating: the most lucrative ladders quickly 'escalate' to substantial sums (10 – 20 – 50 – 250). And the most astute fundraiser will base the request on what you've donated in the past, making the lowest figure 1.5 higher than your previous contribution. Very shrewd. But hey, it's all for a good cause!

DIY experiment

Does this apply only to quick, subconscious and low-stakes decisions? Certainly not. The following scenario is based on an actual experiment:[11]

In court, a prosecutor presents a case before the judge. A driver has caused a collision. The victim, who will be confined to a wheelchair for life, is seeking compensation. The driver's car had failed its MOT and its brakes were defective.

How much would you award in damages?

[£ ....]

Now consider the exact same scenario, but with this addition from the defence team: 'The threshold for appeal is 1,750 pounds.' Again, the question is:

How much would you award in compensation?

[£ ....]

The force of attraction

> In the first case, your answer was probably more than a million pounds.
>
> In the original study, the judges who were presented with the first case awarded, on average, 1.3 million dollars. The second group of judges, who were given the meaningless information about a lower limit for appeal, decided to award the plaintiff 900,000 dollars, nearly half a million less. So clearly the reference effect applies not just to hamburgers, but also to highly educated professionals who are asked to rule on matters of justice and quality of life.

An extremely transparent application of the reference effect comes in the shape of special offers, reductions and closing-down sales. We love those teleshopping channels with their time-limited deals: not 100 pounds, but only 40 pounds until midnight tonight! Does anybody still fall for that these days? US department store chain JCPenney put it to the test. The company hired a new CEO, a heavyweight who'd previously worked at Apple. The tech giant rarely discounts its products, whereas JCPenney had a scattergun approach to leaflets with offers and discount-on-discount vouchers. Anyone who's ever seen the show *Extreme Couponing* knows what we're talking about.* Wasn't it about time to stop this nonsense? The marketing team decided to listen to what consumers had to say and learned that they weren't interested in any of this stuff. Everyday low pricing, that's what they wanted! And that's what they got. It led to change, but not the change that the marketers were hoping for. The new strategy resulted in a 25 percent

---

* If not, have a look on YouTube!

drop in revenue and its market value nearly halved. The coupons are back now, and so are the customers.

The shoppers who were surveyed must have been unable to articulate how they felt: buying a 90-dollar dress for that price is a totally different experience from buying a 180-dollar frock for 90 dollars. That makes sense, because it's often all but impossible to judge the real value of something. When a T-shirt sells for 5 pounds at Primark, but a similar top retails for 150 at the department store across the street, the whole idea of 'reasonable' is up for grabs.

> **Try this at home**
>
> Would you like to have a go at anchoring at home or in the workplace? If so, a useful rhetorical device is paraleipsis. It's the art of professing not to say something while actually saying it. So you might tell someone, 'I obviously can't charge you 10,000 pounds for this' and then give a quote for 5,000 pounds: every word of it is true and it boosts your chances of success. Unfortunately, people often do the exact opposite: 'I really can't do it for free, it's costing me 1,500 pounds in materials alone, so that brings us to 5,000 pounds.' Ouch! Suddenly, that same amount hurts an awful lot more! It's a tactic worth trying in salary negotiations ('I'm not expecting a 25 percent pay rise, but...'), deadlines ('It's really not going to take me a whole year...') or a new TV ('we obviously don't need a 3,000-pound telly...').

The reference effect is also in evidence in a cunning fly buzzing around the aviation sector. Researchers at Washington University analysed twenty years' worth of flight data[12] and noticed that between 1997 and 2017 the same flights seemed to be taking longer and longer. That's to say, the duration mentioned by the airline company when you book increased by more than 8 percent in twenty years. Did planes become slower during this period? Had the maximum air speed been lowered? In their search for an explanation, the analysts whittled it down to a single cause: strategic padding. Landing late is detrimental to your reputation and results in complaints and dissatisfied customers. But rounding up the expected travel time means that the pilot can often report excellent news: we've landed ahead of schedule! Wow, what an amazing carrier. It's also a good strategy to adopt at work: add three days to every deadline and delight your boss again and again. But note that you can't get away with this when you have a colleague who does a similar kind of job. This trick is particularly effective in the absence of alternatives. When another flight is faster, you're going to lose passengers. That would explain why more competition means less strategic padding.

Once upon a time there was a housefly

January 2015, Phoenix, Arizona. Zach Norris discovers a nice old watch in a charity shop. Price: 5.99 dollars. Norris knows a thing or two about timepieces and soon realises that he's chanced upon a vintage Jaeger-LeCoultre Deep Sea Alarm. For the non-connoisseurs among us: a handmade, mechanical Swiss diving watch, which commands prices around 25,000 dollars on the second-hand market. He buys it, obviously. That's when the purchase becomes interesting to us. Norris shares his story on a watch forum, and it goes viral. It's this that makes Zach's find especially attractive to collectors. It has become more valuable because he paid so little for it. In the end, he sells his bargain for an amazing 35,000 dollars plus the watch of his dreams, an Omega Speedmaster. This too is a sought-after model with a great backstory: it was worn by the first astronauts on the moon.

The Housefly Effect

But let's come back down to Earth for a moment. Does a watch become better or more useful for an office worker when it also works in space? Is something really more valuable when a person has picked it up for peanuts? Put differently, have those watch aficionados lost the plot? No. What we're looking at here is simply the housefly effect of an appealing story. Zach's really captured the imagination. Who hasn't dreamed of finding a hidden gem when browsing the stalls at a car boot sale? And astronauts who live or die by the precision of a Swiss watch are the epitome of captivating.

> **DIY experiment**
>
> Auction platform eBay was the site of a fine experiment in story-telling. Having amassed flea-market junk with an average price of 1.25 dollars,[13] journalist Rob Walker decided to find out if a good narrative could inflate the value. He asked professional authors to write fictional narratives to go with each of the items. It worked. A plastic horse's head worth 0.99 dollars sold for no less than 62.95 dollars when it had a nice backstory. In the end Walker resold the stuff he'd bought for 197 dollars for a total of 8,000 dollars!

Stories make things more interesting, an effect we also see in the delightful phenomenon of roadside attractions. When Tim was in Florida, he visited the bizarre Giant Head of Beethoven, as well as a tree that until the mid-twentieth century had been one of the tallest in the state and the swimming pool that *never* counted Edison among its swimmers.* And while on his way to Las Vegas

---

* The same can be said about plenty of pools, but the renowned inventor actually built this one outside his holiday home. He never went in for a splash himself, because he thought exercise was a waste of time.

(for the wedding, remember), he couldn't pass up the chance to see The World's Largest Thermometer. Nondescript places with a storied past that inspire you to make long detours.

Why do narratives inject such appeal? We're made for stories, that's why, and according to certain scholars, we're also shaped by them. What's certain is that humanity began to organise itself more efficiently around the time people learned to tell stories. Legends, myths, sagas: these fictitious tales helped us work together in larger groups. Those who think the appeal of such narratives is a thing of the past might want to consider the huge success of the Marvel films, which are all contemporary retellings of old epics. In some we even see Norse gods such as Thor and Odin coolly drawing large crowds of teenagers (as well as the authors of this book) to the cinema.

Psychologists Carl Jung* and Joseph Campbell did research into the monomyth, the primal story that forms the basis of thousands of narratives around the world and throughout time. You're probably familiar with the hero's journey they encountered everywhere. The protagonist is leading an ordinary life, adventure beckons but he's reluctant, a mentor coaxes him across the threshold, he accepts the challenge, makes friends and foes and enjoys success. Next comes the big test, during which the hero also learns something about himself and is literally or figuratively reborn. A dangerous return journey and an epic final battle are followed by a safe homecoming. Life is back to normal, yet forever changed. Try mapping this template onto your favourite thriller, Homer's *Odyssey* or a nice Pixar film. Or consider the way Donald Trump presented himself as the presidential candidate back in 2016: the hero was safely ensconced in his little wooden hut (ivory tower) in New York, but political adventure beckoned. He notched up

---

* Carl Jung is renowned for the theory of dreams, which is not seen as very scientific. The man could write, though.

success after success, embarked on the perilous journey to the swamp in Washington and, if he were to defeat the Democratic monster, America would be 'great' again.

Never underestimate the impact of a tightly structured story. And vice versa: never underestimate what happens when people aren't fed a ready-made narrative. In 2019, the hijack alarm went off on a plane at Schiphol Airport in Amsterdam. This was literally all the Dutch military police were prepared to share with the public. Nothing else was known at this stage. Within 30 minutes, Twitter users had all but written a thriller about armed attackers issuing demands and panic among the passengers. Then came the denouement: the warning had been triggered by mistake. The lesson from this is that if you fail to give people a story, they'll come up with their own. This is also evident in the many conspiracy theories circulating on the internet. It doesn't take long for a few random observations to cohere into a web of international intrigue, a phenomenon known as **narrative fallacy**.* People are moved by stories, yet policy makers and companies often prefer to communicate through facts. That's hardly surprising, as few of them are gifted novelists and they also have a duty to be transparent and share factual information. Luckily, there are times when the facts are so vivid they're almost a story in their own right. Here's one of the most famous advertising slogans from the *Mad Men* era: 'At 60 miles an hour the loudest noise in the new Rolls-Royce comes from the electric clock.' It's a factual statement but, boy, is it eloquent.

---

* That can't be a coincidence, peeps!

The force of attraction

> **Try this at home**
>
> Want to utilise this effect to move people? You could start with a well-chosen anecdote about, say, dodgy pickup artists or a Swiss watch in a charity shop in Arizona. It's also widely accepted that a moving story about an individual victim often gets more people to dig into their pockets than hard data showing the scale of a problem or an injustice. (Here's another one for your housefly bingo card: the **identifiable victim effect**.) Even just a single sentence can evoke an entire world. The mind fills in the rest. Why not check out some six-word stories? The most famous one is often attributed to Ernest Hemingway: 'For sale: baby shoes, never worn.'*

The housefly on the price tag

I am rich
I deserv[e] it
I am good,
healthy & successful

This was the sole text in the iPhone app *I Am Rich*. Above it shone the kitschy image of a red gem. And that was it. No games, share buttons or hidden Easter eggs. The only interesting thing about this app was its price, 999.99 dollars, the maximum you could charge in the App Store at the time. Did anyone cough up? Oh, yes. The app was bought eight times before Apple removed it from

---

* And why make it as long as six? There are plenty of examples online of five-word stories or less.

its marketplace. At least those who'd clicked on the app by mistake could ask for their money back. Not everybody did, meaning there were people who, purposely, paid nearly a thousand dollars for a few pixels to prove to their friends that they could afford it. Madness, right? Not something you, or anyone you know, would ever do.

OK, let's do a little thought experiment. You're at the car dealership, where two virtually identical mid-range vehicles have caught your eye. Both are comfortable and safe, perform well and are eco-friendly enough. Only one thing sets them apart: their logos. As so often in the automotive industry, this model is marketed under two different brand names. One of them is a bit stuffy, dull and the occasional butt of jokes, the other high-end, reputable and with a bit of a bad-boy image. The price difference is 1,000 pounds... Is it out of the question that – like those who bought *I Am Rich* – you'd shell out a thousand quid for an exclusive emblem? Or do you think you might be tempted?

The same happens with smaller sums of money. Do you pay extra to walk around the sport centre with a *swoosh* on your shirt? Do you think it's not done to serve a supermarket own brand of mineral water at a dinner party? Then maybe you're more like those eight posers than you thought. Never mind. **Status symbols** actually have a very distinct role to play in society. All animals like to flaunt their status as attractive, healthy and strong partners, and this often comes with an element of ostentatious waste. A notable example is the peacock's display of feathers, which makes him a slow-moving target for predators and parasites. A male bird that can afford this must be fast and alert! It's not too dissimilar from the engagement ring that's supposed to cost several months' salary. Or the logo that shows that you have enough disposable income to splash out on T-shirts, watches or handbags.

Companies are constantly trying to make you feel that their product will do for you what feathers do for the peacock. They might join forces with Hollywood stars or influencers, hoping that their wealth and success will rub off on the brand. But celebrities are realising that there's no need to wait for a business to come knocking and are turning themselves into brands. Kanye West sold his famous hip-hop T-shirts for 120 dollars apiece. The power move: they didn't have a logo. Knowing that the loose white tee was an authentic 'Yeezy' would have to be enough. That's good thinking from the rapper. The drive for status is so deeply ingrained in humans that an audience is optional; rich collectors enjoy their Monet or 1960 Fender Stratocaster just as much in isolation. But, of course, it helps if others know what your new purchase is worth. The public outcry over the *I Am Rich* app made it all the more enticing.

This explains why you often see ads for luxury products in less-than-luxurious locations. A very expensive car in a mainstream magazine, for example, or a pricey piece of jewellery on a bus shelter billboard. You'd think these advertisers would have more efficient ways of reaching their target group, and of course they do. But they know full well that a luxury product only becomes truly desirable when your next-door neighbour and brother-in-law are also aware of the price tag. And when you as a potential buyer know that they know.

Companies go to great lengths to heighten that sense of luxury. The remote control of an expensive audio system feels a little heavier. Now you might think that's because of the quality of the components, but no, it simply contains some extra weight so it *feels* better. Likewise, car manufacturers can tell you all there is to know about the sound of closing doors. You don't want it to be plasticky, but heavy and solid, yet not too clunky either. Websites that scan for information or offers make you look unnecessarily long at a progress bar, so you feel their processors are hard at work to give you value for money. The linen napkin in business class, the extra-fancy transparent face masks worn by waiting staff at

The Housefly Effect

Michelin-starred restaurants – all houseflies in expensive clobber.

A phenomenon that we've touched on before often plays a part in this: **scarcity**. Not everything that confers status is scarce, but scarcity can lend status to just about anything. Back in sixteenth-century England, pineapples were extremely rare and therefore a status symbol. Those who weren't in a position to buy their own could hire one – not for consumption, of course, but for display at the dinner table. Sculptures and other representations still adorn the façades of British stately homes. In Japan, meanwhile, where beautiful fruit is seen as a thoughtful gift, you can easily spend 5,000 yen, or 25 pounds, on a nice melon. In 2019, two exceptionally fine specimens sold for as much as 5 million yen. That's a crazy amount of cash. You could buy yourself a fine Rolex for that kind of money, provided the dealer would put you on the waiting list. The Swiss watchmakers, too, know how scarcity works. Recession or not, they get away with raising their prices three times a year and sending non-regular customers packing.

But what to do when your product simply isn't scarce? There are all kinds of ways to make it feel that way. Do you happen to be the only producer of steak pies in Kettering? That means you're the sole purveyor of the 'Authentic Kettering Steak Pie'. Now let's jack up that price. The French have been doing it for years with their cheese and wine, the Brits and Germans with beer: geographical scarcity. Think, too, of first editions, original pressings and numbered print runs: scarcity can be engineered. And that perceived scarcity may well add to the appeal of expensive items. After all, prices go up when demand exceeds supply. But sometimes it works the other way around and products become sought after precisely because they're expensive. Items that sell better when they cost more are known in economic circles as **Veblen goods**. It's a case of reverse price elasticity.

One of Tim's first advertising mentors was approached by a client wanting to sell more luxury sailing trips. Might a

The force of attraction

sophisticated ad do the trick? The advice: 'Double the price and see what happens'. It worked. In no time at all, the vessel was fully booked. And at a large telecom company, Tim learned that customers are more interested in extra services that are *not* free.

It's worth bearing in mind here that the 'price' you pay for something isn't purely monetary. A black belt, a diploma, a pilgrim badge: they're rewards for the effort put in. In circles where conspicuous consumption is frowned upon, there's an equally conspicuous culture of travel, erudition and volunteering. As well as money, those things cost time and effort and take you out of your comfort zone. By doing them you're showing that, like the peacock, you can afford to do so. Some retail chains cleverly exploit this phenomenon, like Lidl with its branded trainers and other merchandise. They're ironic purchases with a serious message, signalling that you're so sure of yourself and your place in the world that you don't need luxury.* Perhaps that's the ultimate luxury.

'Sex sells' – but sometimes no sex is even sexier

The impossible love, the forbidden fruit: we're always drawn to things we're not allowed to do, have or see. It's known as the **Romeo and Juliet effect**, especially in relation to parental opposition to romantic love. The appeal of the illicit was illustrated by a campaign that Tim devised with his colleague Deborah. The two had been asked to promote the sex issue of a parenting magazine. They came up with a fake 'sex tape' featuring their cover star, well-known mother and porn actress Bobbi Eden. But with this twist: Eden and her husband don't do anything in the video, because they're thwarted by their crying baby. In other

---

* See the **red sneakers effect** from chapter 2.

> words, a no-sex tape. All Eden had to do was tweet that she wouldn't be commenting on any leaked footage and the tabloid press was on the line, the 'news' was covered on TV and the magazine had a viral hit on their hands. According to the Internet Adult Film Database (the most decent source we were able to find), Eden can be seen in (explicit) action in no fewer than 188 films. But the one video that people weren't supposed to watch was a lot more interesting, even though she kept her dressing gown on.

In summary: the power of attention (and repetition)

Now you've seen which houseflies you can harness to make your good cause, your company, your idea or indeed yourself more attractive. Start by making sure you stand out, perhaps by being different from those around you (Von Restorff effect). Be kind (always a good approach) and identify common ground. Remember that framing isn't just something spin doctors do, but a common housefly that can be found buzzing around your home too. The technique revolves around a simple question: what lens do you want people to look through? You've read about the huge influence of a well-chosen comparison: anchoring, or the reference effect. And perhaps you've experimented with a clever paraleipsis: 'I obviously can't charge you 1,000 pounds for this.' You've read that a compelling story can be a massive housefly. And you'll remember that it's better to focus on a single victim than on the big picture (the identifiable victim effect). Veblen goods have shown you that you can make something more attractive by charging more for it. And if you're wondering why we're reiterating all this, then you haven't been paying attention. Remember we told you that repetition can make something extra appealing with the help of two flies called mere exposure and processing fluency? Oh, and if you're planning on going out on the town soon, leave the dryer lint at home. That cutie you've got your eye on will have read *The Housefly Effect* too.

> The incentive fly often heads in unexpected directions.

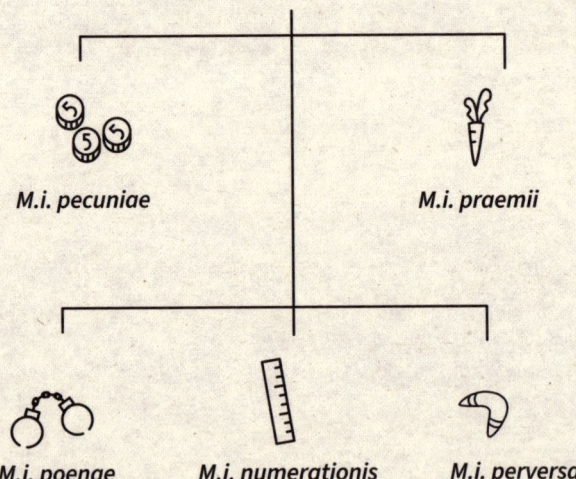

Chapter 7
Money and motivation, punishment and penalties

Musca incentivae or 'incentive fly'

Subspecies: *M.i. pecuniae* (financial incentive), *M.i. praemii* (reward), *M.i. poenae* (punishment), *M.i. numerationis* (measure), *M.i. perversa* (perverse incentive)

Big fat effective fly with a sting, often the first to spring to mind when we think of houseflies, but that sting is often overestimated and tends not to last as long as expected.

Application: note, stick to the recommended dose, and distribute evenly, otherwise the effect of *M. incentivae* can turn against you.

Carrot and stick

When India was still a British colony, Delhi was ravaged by a plague of snakes. These weren't just any old snakes, they were dangerous, venomous cobras. So the government intervened with its favourite tool: rewards. Anyone who captured a cobra received a handsome sum. Did it work? At first. A great many of the hissing monsters were captured, but soon the impoverished population realised that breeding cobras and handing them in could generate a handy additional income stream. Not a disaster in itself, albeit not the intention. Things only went badly wrong when the government became aware of the scheme and abruptly ended its snake programme. The population had no option but to release all those cobras they'd bred, leaving Delhi with more cobras than it started with.

This phenomenon, the well-intended incentive that works out all wrong, has since become known as the **cobra effect**, an example of *Musca incentivae perversa*. At the end of this book we'd like to take a closer look at these unintended side effects, as with all these tricks, techniques, phenomena and effects, you might be wondering: isn't there a simpler way? Rewards, punishments, liberal use of penalties and bonuses, these often seem the simplest, most direct ways to steer behaviour, but it's precisely here that flies often buzz off in unexpected directions. We'll reveal the extent to which your intuition lets you down, using a number of fascinating studies.

Money often isn't the best motivator and this fly is adorned with venomous spikes. If you pay someone too little (or less than others), you run the risk of mutiny – or even detrimental effects on employee health. When you suddenly offer money for something people were already motivated to do, fewer of them exhibit the desired behaviour, rather than more, and financial rewards can do more harm than good. Palaeontologists discovered this the hard way: when Gustav Königswald, a nineteenth-century explorer, offered the population money for every piece of human skull on Java, he had to piece the broken shards back together himself.[1]

This chapter looks at the most significant effects of both tangible and intangible carrots and sticks. How do you reward someone for work? By unit, per hour, with bonuses – all of those are possibilities, as long as you think carefully about the precise behaviour you want to reward. Alongside money, compliments or scores are effective rewards that ensure that we exhibit the desired behaviour more frequently. The form this takes is important; the reward has to be 'incentive-compatible' or, in other words, those who work harder should earn more money. Yet Eva doesn't give her cleaner bonuses, nor does she pay her mother-in-law for childcare, while Tim is highly motivated to provide free advertising for his band. Clearly there's a limit to how much motivation you can generate with money.

The same is true on a larger scale. If you ask someone in the Western world whether they work for money alone, only 20 percent say yes.*[2] The satisfaction people experience in a job is also reflected in macro-economic figures. When tax on income or assets rises,

---

* The 'bullshit job' (or 'socially useless job') is a well-known and ubiquitous phenomenon.

for instance, rich people don't instantly start working less. Poor people also don't stop looking for work when they receive welfare payments or basic income, sometimes not even when working means earning *less*, and when they're not required to apply for jobs. Clearly rewards are slippery flies – sometimes necessary, sometimes superfluous, sometimes even counterproductive. This chapter will teach you when they do work.

Educational bonuses

Knowledge is power, and the act of measurement arms us with knowledge. This applies both in economics and in marketing. In education too, tests are an important way of establishing performance. In the Netherlands schools are chosen and subsidies awarded based on standardised testing known as CITO. Scores in all subjects have been dropping gradually since 2003, in comparison with other countries as well. In 2019 literacy even dropped below the OECD average.*

Well, you might be wondering if this is down to teachers' salaries. In part the low scores will be because Dutch teachers are poorly paid, but a more surprising explanation is that the students are paid too little for their achievements. What happens when you reward students for a high grade in their maths test?

It sounds odd, but it's a workable way of investigating whether the motivation of school students is the same in different cultures. Researchers gave some of the students in schools in Shanghai and the US a reward when they did well.[3] The students were only told just before the test, so it couldn't have been down to studying harder in advance. The American students who received a reward put in much higher levels of extra effort, so much so that the US

---

* The Organisation for Economic Co-operation and Development, a club of 38 rich countries.

would have shifted from thirty-sixth place to nineteenth in the world ranking if students throughout the country were rewarded. The Shanghai students, however, didn't score any better. Clearly, they were already so motivated that the money had little effect on their performance. There are two lessons to learn here: firstly, Dutch students may be insufficiently motivated for their tests; and secondly, rewards only work when there's room for improvement.

And those teachers, do they have room for improvement? Schools, especially in developing countries, have been trying for years to work out what makes teachers more productive, i.e. better at teaching. The first condition is the teachers' presence, quite apart from what they do. In developing countries that's not a given. In India, for example, a bonus system reduced truancy – by the teachers themselves.[4] (An incentive worked better here than with those snakes.) A second step is to reward teachers for how much they teach students. In the Netherlands that would be a sensitive area, as teachers aren't seen as lacking drive or commitment. For the workshy American teachers from the documentary *Waiting for Superman* (2010), a bonus for the number of children who learn to read seems more appropriate. The teachers generally do turn up, but some teach so poorly that students leave school virtually illiterate.

Those bonuses didn't work in education, though, at least not in America. More was needed to boost these teachers' morale. In 2014 two economists from the University of Chicago, John List and Steven Levitt (of *Freakonomics*), unleashed a dirty housefly (you'll remember from chapter 3): they took money away. Armed with money from donors, List and Levitt wanted one last try at a study into the efficacy of bonuses. They divided schools into two groups at random. In one group teachers could earn an old-fashioned end-of-year bonus of up to 8,000 dollars, based on their students' academic performance. At other schools the teachers received 4,000 dollars at the *beginning* of the school year. If their students did well, they could earn up to 8,000 dollars in total, but if their students had progressed less than the others, they had to pay back the initial lump sum. Progress was measured in relative terms, so teachers from both groups achieving the same class score would earn the same overall bonus.

Both common sense and the traditional economist would say, same incentive, so probably the same result, yet the difference was significant. Teachers paid in advance saw their students perform considerably better. Those students had 10 percent better grades in maths and comprehension than the other group, while the old-fashioned bonuses had no effect whatsoever on student performance. A sceptical reader might think that teachers who receive money for high grades would turn a blind eye if their weak students cheated, but the students also scored 13 percent higher at the state-wide tests in *all* subjects, while those results fell outside the remit of the study.[5]

So bonuses in education sometimes work, as long as they're targeted at students and particularly where there's plenty of room for improvement; taking bonuses away works even better. This is promising for bonuses in jobs where people are less intrinsically motivated, where they have even more impact.

Sick bonuses

In 1934 a law was passed in America that made it compulsory to publicise the CEO's salary. That was sure to curb self-enrichment, they thought. In 2016 a researcher, armed with modern data analysis tools, set out to see if it had worked. His conclusion: owing to the transparency, the CEOs' salaries had in fact risen faster than others. It wasn't the top dog who earned a little more who felt ashamed, but actually those left dangling below, and as a board of directors you're not exactly going to impress with a cheap and cheerful CEO.[6]

In 2015 the Dutch financial sector introduced a bonus ceiling of a maximum of 20 percent of the regular salary. There were political reasons for this – after the crisis people felt that bankers should make decisions consistent with the long-term interest of the bank, not their end-of-year bonus. Bringing in extra clients under false pretences turned out to have serious consequences. Things had to reach crisis point for a bonus ceiling to be established, when in fact in 2008 it had been demonstrated in the lab, so to speak, that bonuses were bad for people's motivation and performance. As soon as there is the slightest modicum of thinking required for the task, the higher the bonus, the worse the performance became.[7] A drawback of giving a bonus to the best employee is that there are generally more people who miss out. Chapter 3 showed us that those people suffer more than the winner enjoys winning. What happens when someone feels undervalued? They stop trying so hard.[8]

Most politicians will worry first and foremost about loss of productivity, but even employees' health suffers from an unfair salary, as shown in a Swiss experiment.[9] People were tasked with counting how frequently the number 1 appeared on pages filled with numbers. Participants received 3 euros when they tallied up the right number of 1s on a page. If they made a single mistake, they only received 1 euro, and nothing at all for two or more errors. In twenty-five stressful minutes, the average participant earned 21 euros.

The researchers also built a sting into the tail in the manner of payment. They didn't pay the wages directly to the hard worker, but to another participant, who as the 'employer' had to decide how much to relinquish to their 'employee'. On average the employees received only 9.50 euros from their 'employers' – less than half. Would you put up with that? For some it was more or less what they expected of an employer, but most anticipated receiving far more. Their pulse and heart-rate variability were recorded from the moment they heard how much they would earn, and those who felt exploited exhibited less healthy patterns, known to potentially lead to heart problems.

> **Fly against the glass ceiling**
>
> Does fair reward systematically backfire? It certainly does – in the case of the pay gap between men and women. In the Netherlands 7 percent of women's wages disappears into that gap, when correcting for part-time work and age structure. (Now you'll be wondering why men are more prone to cardiovascular disease.) But you'll be relieved to read that there are things you can do about it.
>
> 1. Do you want to treat women and men equally? Then state explicitly in a job ad that the salary can be negotiated – otherwise men do so and women don't. See chapter 1 on self-deception.
>
> 2. Do you want more women to put themselves forward for high-flying positions? Then leave the vacancy open longer – women take more time to decide whether to apply.
>
> 3. Do you want to appoint more women to high positions? Make sure you have a list of women to choose from, or evaluate candidates on particular skills.
>
> 4. Would you like more of these kinds of evidence-based tips? Read *What Works* by Iris Bohnet.[10]

In the long term the feeling of being exploited (or underpaid) leads to stress, cardiovascular disease and other health issues. The same researchers therefore examined data on health, income, education and age from 25,000 German citizens since 1984. The data confirmed that people who felt they were paid too little were in worse physical shape, even when they took into account objective income, education, the labour market and type of job. In fact, this led to typical stress-related symptoms, particularly among employees over fifty. The moral of the story: make sure you pay your employees enough, and don't give one more than another.

But watch out. Rewards can also backfire. In 1908 *The New York Times* published an article about a dog that chased children into the River Seine, in order to rescue them afterwards. It emerged that he was rewarded with a steak when he walked by the butcher's with a wet child. This was clearly a case of too high a reward. The opposite also occurs. Blood donors generally aren't rewarded, but give blood because they see the need and value of it (much like Eva's mother-in-law caring for her grandson out of love). A blood bank in Sweden[11] nevertheless wanted to show their appreciation for the volunteers and started paying some of them 7 dollars. It made an enormous difference. The group that received the reward donated half as much blood.

What was going on here? People were already motivated to give blood. By offering money, the blood bank made it clear what the blood was worth to them, and that turned out to be less than the volunteers themselves considered worthwhile. To some of the people those 7 dollars felt insulting. The phenomenon is termed a **displacement effect** on intrinsic motivation. Fortunately the solution for the blood bank was already baked into the experiment. The other group were offered the 7 dollars, along with the opportunity to donate it to a good cause. This completely eradicated the effect.

Money stinks

So bonuses lead to unhealthy bankers and poor performance. But there was an additional cause of the financial crisis: the business climate itself turned out to be a housefly. Now you're thinking, this is about bankers, not about me, but it really is about you. Do you have to pay for coffee at work? Then it's likely that more pens and printer paper are stolen at your company, not to mention other unethical behaviour playing out on the work floor, such as fraud, corruption and harassment. A recent study[12] (see the box below) shows that the mere thought of money is an important trigger for stealing and lying.

> **Lying for money**
>
> Imagine taking part in a study in which someone asks you to lie for money. You're in contact with another participant on a chat screen. You're rewarded with 5 euros if you claim you received less money than the other person, who then gets 2 euros. If you refuse to lie, you receive 2 euros and the other 5. What would you do?
>
> But wait. Before you present this dilemma to others, you first make your participants think of money. You could use a silly puzzle, for example: 'You have two coins that together are worth 15 cents. One is *not* a 5-cent coin. What's the other?'
>
> This experiment has been conducted several times, for real money. When participants were primed to think of money in advance, they were twice as likely to lie and pocket the 5 euros. Of course all the players were in it for the money, but why should 'warming up' with financial thoughts cause more unethical behaviour? (See also chapter 1 on priming.) What do you think? Perhaps the thought of cash triggers competitiveness, or the desire for power or financial

> independence. But money seems to invoke a very specific reaction: a business-like approach, which in turn suppresses our capacity to empathise. Just think of Michael Corleone in *The Godfather*, saying to his brother, 'It's nothing personal – it's strictly business.'[13]*

Unethical behaviour in the workplace leads to as much as a 5 percent loss for companies,† so it's a very real effect. The painful conclusion is that money itself is the housefly that pushes people to be more selfish. And which professions provide the most space for unethical behaviour? Precisely, those in which money plays an important role, as in the case of stockbrokers and checkout workers. If there were less emphasis on money (and more on, say, service), it might lead to better behaviour among such employees, but the discovery that money itself triggers dishonesty has consequences for the way all companies conduct their business: asking staff to pay for lunch or coffee by card reduces exposure to physical money and calculations. So there's room for easy improvement to the business climate.

How does this apply to banks? Was it a culture of greed that caused the crisis? That was only a putative accusation, until a follow-up study was published in 2014.[14] Bank employees were asked to toss a coin ten times. Depending on whether they reported heads or tails, they were given 20 dollars or nothing. To reflect the competitive environment in a bank, they were only paid if they earned more than a random other person. One group of bankers had filled in a questionnaire beforehand about TV programmes. This group

---

* Even completely ordinary study participants turned out to be more willing to kill a mouse if it was a 'side effect' of a market transaction than if it was an individual decision.
† According to ACFE, the Association of Certified Fraud Examiners.

was slightly dishonest on average: they reported throwing heads 51 percent of the time, which might just be coincidence. The second group received a survey that was mainly about the bank, strongly reminding them of their 'bank identity'. These bankers claimed on average that they had thrown heads 58 percent of the time, which isn't very likely. A relatively benign explanation might be that they thought of money when reminded of the bank, and that this triggered the dishonest effect. Disappointingly, that's not it. When the experiment, including the two different surveys, was repeated among students, neither group was more dishonest, suggesting that it was the business climate that was the culprit here.

What can we do about it? Serving free coffee didn't help here. Encouraging conversations to reflect on the culture, perhaps? That's precisely what another follow-up study did. Researchers implemented a two-month 'ethical programme', after which mystery shoppers dropped by to see whether the participating employees had grown more honest. They presented themselves as ordinary customers and asked which financial products might be appropriate for them, mentioning a number of products that were profitable for the bank but less so for the customer. Sadly, the bankers weren't any more honest. If anything, the programme had a negative effect – clearly the bad guys had more of an influence on the good guys than vice versa.* Or alternatively, this kind of subconscious housefly effect is hard to remedy by talking. What's needed is changes to reward structures and the environment.

Carrots as sticks: taxes, penalties and compensation

Now we know that the carrot – extra money – has remarkable side effects. What about the stick? Among the teachers whose bonus

---

* See also chapter 4 on the social housefly.

was taken away, the stick appeared to have more effect than the carrot.

The government uses both to steer our behaviour: taxes, penalties and surcharges. Taxes are primarily intended for collecting money, and penalties to change behaviour, of course, but it's only in the last twenty years that people have systematically examined their effect on behaviour. This has provided a number of lessons.

Taxes lead to behavioural change when they're high, visible and preferably introduced abruptly. Small, slow price rises, as with food or cigarettes, achieve relatively little, but when it comes to luxury goods (the Veblen goods discussed in chapter 6), higher tax is often far more effective. People want a car that's bigger than their neighbour's, not a large car per se. In part it's about projecting an image, in part it's a rational safety concern: the occupants of the tallest and heaviest car have the greatest survival chance in a crash. If everyone has to pay a bit more for a heavier car, the relative prices of your car and the neighbour's remain the same, but in total there are slightly fewer deaths because fewer people buy heavier cars.

Another way in which tax is deployed to save lives is via a more circuitous route. Obesity is a significant problem in the UK (almost 30 percent of Brits suffer from this condition). The government recently decided to levy a tax on soft drinks containing sugar. Rather than charging 1p more per gram of sugar, they used thresholds: all drinks with more than 5 grams of sugar per litre cost 18 pence more, and those with over 8 grams cost 24 pence more. The result was not so much that consumers bought far less cola as that soft drinks manufacturers anxiously kept their beverages under the threshold, fearing that consumers would be sensitive to the price rise. The tax therefore indirectly had an enormous effect, as almost all soft drinks now contain less sugar. A double nudge!

Penalties, in contrast to tax, are intended to adjust behaviour. This can sometimes end in epic failure. For Eva every working day is a ticking time bomb: her child has to be picked up from nursery before half past six, on penalty of scathing looks, a humiliated and hungry child and, in the worst-case scenario, the police. For nursery workers, late parents are a daily irritation.

In 1998 Uri Gneezy,[15] an Israeli economist, arrived late for nursery pickup for the umpteenth time. He sat down with the nursery owners and considered the problem: they wanted to fine parents for being late. In order to compare results, six of the ten nurseries in the chain introduced the fine: 10 shekels for every ten minutes, which equates to just over 3 pounds in today's money. They waited, rubbing their hands in glee on the first day to see the results.

In the ten weeks that followed there was an explosion of latecomers, because yes, if you can just make your point in the meeting for another 3 pounds, it's a no-brainer. The effect of the penalty was that people made a rational calculation, instead of seeing half past six as a hard deadline. Worse than that, after ten weeks, when the furious owner lifted the fines, just as many parents continued to arrive late. They now knew they could pay off their behaviour; the social norm had been undermined by the market norm.

Sorry, but apologies don't (always) work

What if you've done something wrong and want to apologise? A little cash can give your sincere apologies extra force, but don't just throw money at the problem. Say you've ordered an Uber, which doesn't turn up or is more than five minutes late. That has an effect on the company – customers subsequently use the app 5 to 10 percent less, so the company sent automatically generated emails saying 'sorry, sorry, sorry' in response to bad reviews. Sadly those deeply felt apologies didn't help. Uber

Money and motivation, punishment and penalties

> called on a famous economist, John List, mentioned above, to find out what the best 'sorry strategy' might be. He set off experimenting with his team: thousands of customers received differently worded emails and thousands were offered money on top in the form of a 5-dollar voucher. What did they find out? People reacted far better to the voucher than to apologies. So well, in fact, that they went on to make more use of the app, which made it very much worth the effort for Uber to continue handing out these little gifts. But when the customers had several bad experiences in a row, the vouchers did more harm than good: then they were perceived as a sign of incompetence.[16]

The lesson from this famous experiment in the nurseries is that fines should be coupled with social censure – they should bring down someone's status and reinforce the norm. Or they should simply cause great financial suffering. Otherwise both rewards and penalties can work very perversely indeed.

Measurement is a fat fly

Solicitors' offices are home to enormous houseflies. People fight over them, they're grabbed from the hands of couriers and hidden, the boss claims them, even when the interns have done most of the work: tombstones, Plexiglass or bronze statues with a logo, which are given to the offices to celebrate a large takeover or acquisition. Men over sixty earning six- or seven-figure salaries cherish these tombstones as trophies. Symbolic rewards, punishments, compliments and frowns are often at least as powerful as monetary equivalents. Rankings, badges, savings schemes, stickers, an extra retweet or like on social media, all get the dopamine flowing. It's precisely because we react so strongly to it that the way feedback is given is so sensitive. Feedback must take the right form, at the right moment and in the right dose.

You've almost finished this book now. Say you want to do something useful with the knowledge you've picked up. How would you get an airline to save fuel? Yes, raising tax on kerosene* is sure to work, and there are another three levers you can pull. Pilots decide how much fuel to take, based on weather predictions and the weight of the aircraft – taking too much leads to extra fuel consumption. Like drivers, they can have a more or less thrifty flying style, and finally after landing they can taxi more or less sparingly.

Now you're thinking: old-fashioned punishment or reward? Hang posters in the pilots' changing rooms saying 'I FLY ECONOMICALLY'? Teaching seasoned professionals new tricks is pretty challenging. Researchers thought that a teaching method involving measurement and immediate feedback might work. They divided 335 pilots into four groups. One group was only told that there was an experiment running on energy usage. The other three groups received a monthly letter informing them of their personal performance in terms of energy-efficient flying. Some were given targets and received 17 dollars towards a good cause if they achieved them.

The researchers had hypothesised that rewards, even if destined for a good cause rather than the participant, would deliver the greatest effect on energy saving. That turned out not to be the case – the group given targets without a reward, for example, switched off one of the engines during taxiing 8 percent more frequently than the control group. An additional reward made no difference to that, although pilots were 6 percent happier for it, which was a nice side effect. But the nicest thing was that even the group who

---

* Simply introducing a tax would be a good start: there's currently no tax on kerosene.

received no feedback flew more economically, probably because they felt like they were being watched – an effect often observed. In this case the pilots from all groups continued to fly more efficiently, even after the study ended. The saving was as much as 550 kilos of fuel per flight. For a single airline (Virgin Atlantic), that adds up to 21 million kilos less CO_2 emissions (or five million dollars in fuel costs).

This kind of benefit can also be achieved at home, albeit in more modest figures. For several years now some energy companies have included feedback on energy consumption in bills. Did you use more or less this month than a year ago, than the neighbours, than an average household? The information they display isn't just plucked out of thin air. In 2007, Opower, an American energy company, became the first to conduct systematic research into how you can use billing data to persuade people to reduce their energy consumption. Their primary trick was the combination of social norms with personalised feedback. In practice, it looks like this:

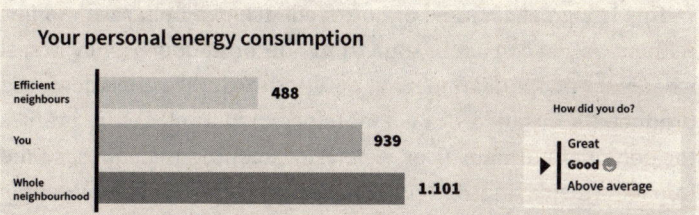

There are a number of houseflies lurking in this.

A. Say someone scores better than average, as in this case. Of course you don't want that person to read the message, 'You're already outperforming your neighbours.' Effectively, there always needs to be someone doing better.

B. The reverse is also true: if you show someone that they're doing badly, it's easy to fall into thinking, 'You see, I'm the kind of person who can't do this' (the negative little brother of the attribution housefly in chapter 1). That's why the overview always included a group performing worse than the recipient.

C. An extra compliment for the right behaviour turned out to offer a substantial boost. When Opower threw in some smileys (see image above), the results were even better: on average people saved 2 percent of their energy per household, adding up to 2 billion dollars.[17]

The energy company reached this conclusion by conducting thousands of experiments with the way feedback was displayed. Likewise, Booking.com uses feedback to get the best out of their employees (until they burn out) and Uber uses it to get their drivers to keep driving.

This is a great example of how feedback can help save money. As soon as you can count something – information, money, steps, whatever – people start to make comparisons. Take gross domestic product, for instance, or on a more personal level, Tinder profiles for potential partners, user reviews of washing machines, or the impact of displaying total spending on the number of items people chucked into their shopping trolley. But because they're so easy to compare, numbers are also very deceptive. What do people do with their step counter? They shake it. What do companies do on social media? They buy followers.* What do doctors do when they're rewarded for successful operations? They avoid difficult

---

* Course we do! *The Housefly Effect* bought up a load of fake profiles on Instagram. Within a week that brought us 1/10 of that number in additional real followers. Were you one of them?

ones. In other words, it's really useful to measure things, especially in hospitals, but as soon as you pair it with rewards, even just compliments, you instantly overshoot the goal. This phenomenon is known as **Goodhart's Law**: when something is measured, people act on it, but as we've seen, when a measure becomes a target, it ceases to be a good measure. See also the snakes mentioned in the introduction to this chapter.

Go figure

So numbers have a huge influence on your behaviour. Run through the numbers you've seen in the past hour: retweets, fuel consumption, Air Miles, number of unread emails, etc. What effect do these numbers have on you? Did you choose this feedback, or was it designed by someone else? Reflect on what behaviour each number encourages, what you're comparing your score to and when you get to see the figures. Twitter and Facebook, for instance, have experimented with less addictive versions of their app. Their revolutionary change was to display fewer figures.

Does money work?

The short answer is, of course it does. People run faster if you pay them more. Literally, it turns out, as shown in the salary data of 487 footballers. Two Swiss economists decided what would constitute a 'fair' salary for all players in the Bundesliga, based on observations by experts. They compared that with the market value of players that season, which is approximately equivalent to their actual salary. Overvalued footballers in fact really did work harder to give their best. It seemed as if they were applying some kind of one-good-turn-deserves-another rule. Conversely, for footballers who received lower than 'appropriate' remuneration, every percentage point lower wage resulted in proportionally less hard work on the pitch.[18]

Rewards are ubiquitous houseflies, but tend to be overestimated. How do you design an incentive to get your colleague (or child, or customer) to work as hard as possible? Checklist:

1. Look at whether they're already exhibiting the desired behaviour (child clearing the table, parents arriving on time, donors giving blood). If so, don't give them money!

2. Is only the result measurable (as in many work situations)? Then reward that result, preferably with compliments.

3. Is the link between effort and result clear (hard-working teachers, for example)? Is the effort measurable? Then reward effort.

4. Consider what will happen when people do what you're incentivising them to do (think of the snakes).

And finally, if you're looking at team results in which individual efforts are unclear, or tasks change over time, or if both effort and result are unmeasurable, stay well away from financial rewards. The rest of the book may be more useful in such cases, because really almost any other way of getting someone to do something is preferable.

Epilogue

You've now met a great many houseflies. Some of them may have made you feel angry or alarmed at the ruthless effectiveness with which houseflies send people off the rails, unintentionally or as a result of deliberate manipulation. Perhaps you resolved never again to allow yourself to be controlled by certain houseflies, and you remembered to tell people about them at work. Hopefully, sometimes they made you smile, because you recognised yourself in the effects, because let's be honest, they make us human. The housefly, rather than the dog, was probably our very first pet.

Often these effects also make life more fun. If you decide to go on that world trip and it's great, what does it matter if you did it because of those clumsy Booking.com flies? If you danced the night away with your new date despite your early-morning appointment, does it matter that it happened as a result of **hyperbolic discounting**? Of course not. In fact, perhaps you're itching to use all those effects to give yourself or someone else that little nudge in the right direction. We'd love that. However, we also feel responsible. Aren't we effectively handing out loaded weapons in the street here? Actually, it's not that bad; at the end of the day, we humans remain gloriously stubborn, even with all those flies. Nevertheless, we'd like to give you the following advice.

So you want to use a housefly

First of all, the thorny ethical question: is it okay to do this? Shouldn't we regulate which houseflies we apply and how?

Cass Sunstein, one of the authors of *Nudge*, mentions three ethical considerations in applying houseflies.* First is the stakes involved. Many houseflies are targeted at relatively innocent choices. Our environment is designed, so it makes sense for the designers to be aware of the effect of their work – as long as freedom of choice is preserved, it's okay to try to tempt people to buy a bunch of flowers. But sometimes houseflies are far from innocent, even if freedom of choice is maintained. In a referendum, the way the choices are worded and the order in which they're presented influences how people vote, but we often don't know the magnitude of that influence.

Besides the interest at stake and the irreversibility of a choice, it's important to consider whether someone is happy to be nudged. In order to decide that, you can ask yourself: if you had the choice to deploy the housefly on a loved one, would you do it? If so, then there's a good chance it's ethically acceptable. If the housefly is plainly visible, and therefore easy to avoid, it's hard to argue against it.

We can spend entire evenings debating this, drink in hand. Eva might claim that the government should ensure subscriptions aren't extended by default, to which Tim may respond by wondering how pleasant it would really be to have to extend your phone, internet, gas, electricity, insurance, Netflix and Spotify contracts every single month. Or Eva will tease Tim about the less savoury customers he's advised over the course of his career. Does his work for good causes provide karmic compensation, or should he have said no to some clients selling products such as sugar or alcohol?

---

* Sunstein has formulated a 'Bill of Rights for Nudging', in which he sets out the ethical boundaries of using houseflies.

In response to which Tim tells her about a surgeon friend whom he asked if there were people she wouldn't want to operate on. What if you saved a serious criminal who went on to commit murder? The ethical discussion made little impression on the doctor: everyone deserves medical care, end of. Well then, thought Tim, why doesn't everyone deserve a promo video?

Eva gets more worked up about the opposite: people make far too little use of houseflies. Countless organisations strive for wonderful causes but are too honest to deliberately deploy these techniques. How ethical is it *not* to save the world because you refuse to use effective methods? She cites the example of the climate crisis. A swarm of houseflies prevents us from properly tackling the problem. Eva sums them up as follows: living a climate-neutral life is in the present, the reward in the future (present bias), and we receive barely any feedback on our efforts. Climate change happens gradually, so we get used to it and don't notice. Social proof also works against you, because buying something or going somewhere is always more visible than not doing so. Even the sucker effect plays a role: are you about to become the only idiot who actually stays home while everyone else keeps on happily flying around the world? Meanwhile everyone's still looking at this problem through the carefully established frame of 'climate change', which invokes far less panic than a term such as 'global catastrophe'. That's where Tim and Eva can agree: if we want to solve these kinds of problems, we can't afford to ignore housefly effects.

Try it out for yourself

In the introduction we started out with a disclaimer: don't launch into brain surgery with this book in hand. Now that you've seen all these houseflies and their effects, you know there's no such thing as *the* housefly effect. We tested out a number of variants of the original Dutch edition of this book to see which cover was most attractive. We'd like to have done that in bookshops, as all those flies have individual effects and, worse still, they're context-dependent. So how do you apply this new knowledge?

Say you'd like your housemates to turn the light off when they go out. You *could* open up a jar of flies, pick out your favourite and see what happens, but it's smarter to follow the step-by-step plan below.

Step-by-step plan for successful housefly effect

1. What result are you aiming for?	Lower energy bill (Saskia switches the light off as she goes out of the door.)
2. Draw a picture of the behaviour required; who needs to do what when	
3. How can you measure whether things are improving? Write down what you're going to count, when and for how long.	Table of number of times the light is out when you come home.
4. Put yourself in Saskia's place (in the drawing, physically, or talk to her). Does she not want to? Is she unable to? Or does it not occur to her?	It slips her mind because she's preoccupied with her child.
5. See if you can make the behaviour easier (chapter 2), more attractive (chapters 3, 6, 7), more sociable (chapter 4) or timely (chapter 5).	More sociable/appealing: get the child to press the button by giving it a sound effect.
6. Try it out for a bit and watch out for side effects!	8 x out of 14 days the light was off, neighbours complaining about noise
7. Happy? If not, back to step 5!	5

Epilogue

Now you're getting down to work, in the office perhaps, with respectable houseflies that deprive people of nothing and only help them make better choices. It can still make people feel a bit weird when they realise you've been using them as guinea pigs. For instance, what were your thoughts when you read that the book's cover had been tested for attractiveness? Lots of people complained that making face masks compulsory during the pandemic was part of a behavioural experiment. Meanwhile people were happy enough to participate in the multitude of behavioural experiments *every day* on Amazon. Experiments are part of public life. From political to commercial Facebook ads, from the format of *The Farmer Wants a Wife* to bills, every adjustment is tested. Even as a citizen of your country of residence, you're a guinea pig, and why not, if experiments teach us what people want and do?

Measuring is essential for gaining that knowledge, and if you start measuring you may find that the effect of a housefly can be enormous. But what constitutes enormous? You might say you've taken a successful approach when you get an improvement of 4 percent. Is that a lot? It is in practice. In loads of cases, after all, the winner takes all. Whether you're selling toilet paper or standing as a candidate for president of the United States, if you're just a little more effective than the competition, you've won. A manufacturer who sells 4 percent more of a product might be eligible for marketing awards and a nice promotion. The percentages can also add up or even multiply. An experiment in the Rotterdam metro revealed that a mixture of more attractive lighting, pleasant music and a fresh scent made travellers happier. Something similar can happen when you improve your website a little: a little social evidence here, a good story there and a temporary offer of a limited edition, for example. So don't just test each factor separately, try them in combination too.

Finally

A single unified model of human behaviour doesn't exist. So don't see the effects in this book as formulas that will always be successful, but as glimpses that will bring you closer to the truth. Housefly effects can be larger or smaller, robust or somewhat mysterious, temporary or permanent, but reading about them helps you look at things, such as your own behaviour and that of the people around you, from different angles. If that happens, as far as we're concerned this book has been a success, and if you feel that way, please share it on social media with #houseflyeffect. If you want, of course – it's entirely your choice!*

---

* Of course we end on a housefly effect. This one's called the BYAF or **but-you-are-free effect**: emphasise that people have freedom of choice and there's a higher chance they'll do what you ask. But you saw that coming, right?

Acknowledgements

First and foremost we want to thank Anna Asbury and Laura Vroomen, the translators, for adding just that bit of British *je ne sais quoi* to out Dutch wordings, and Jamie Hodder-Williams, Polly Halsey and Chella Busch for turning this edition into reality. Without Sander Ruys of Maven Publishing, who brought us together, you wouldn't be holding this book now. We're grateful to our literary agent Willem Bisseling and the entire team at Sebes & Bisseling for their mediation and good advice – without them we would have ended up with a blog, at best. Renée Deurloo and the team at Spectrum made our idea into a book. Renée, Mark Bogema, Kees Noorda, Léon Groen: thank you for the great collaboration!

We're also extremely grateful to our initial set of benevolently critical readers. Joost van Gelder, Lisa Becking and Menno Schilthuizen: thanks for helping us develop our fly family tree. Joël van der Weele, Wilte Zijlstra, Jona Linde, Joris Gillet, Job Harms, Karin Bongers, Floris Heukelom, Hannah Schmidberger and, above all, Alien van der Vliet did us an immense service, using their technical knowledge to take various chapters to the next level.

Yvette van der Meer's advice on copy edits made many sentences flow ~~just that little bit~~ better. Bas Erlings helped us practise what we preach with consumer research into the most effective subtitle and cover for the original Dutch edition. Speaking of which, our cover design had to be developed with knowledge of housefly effects and no one is better at that than Deborah Bosboom. Thank you!

Finally, of course, all those crude oversimplifications, disputed studies and circuitous sentences we've left in are our own responsibility. Even we're not immune to an infamous fly like the IKEA effect.*

Personal note from Eva
Tim, working with you has opened my eyes: to how sexy this topic is, to how much more light-heartedly I can write about it, to the power of a well-targeted conjunction. What a pleasure it is when someone instantly gets what you mean, yet has completely different examples to add. The lockdown writing process became almost a game for me, punctuated by your WhatsApp messages delivering harsh observations and lightning-speed connections. What the hell, maybe I really will get a housefly tattoo for the third print run – to remind me how wonderful it is to work with you.

I dedicate this book to my parents, who made up booklets and stories with me, and my teachers Ger Kleis, Menno Lievers and Peter Todd, who taught me how to deal with criticism.

Personal note from Tim
Eva, writing a book is supposed to be an ordeal, isolating yourself in a garret, wrestling with the empty page and the bottle. How different it was to write this book with you. A weekly party filled with insights and studies that I felt instantly compelled to share with others. Thanks for the verbal jam sessions, the private lectures and your structure over my chaos. If the reader learns half as much from this book as I did from you, it's a resounding success. Time for another sequel?

I dedicate this book to my mother, who was a writer, my wife, who is a writer and my daughter, who wants to become one. And to my father because without him...

---

* A cognitive bias whereby people place a higher value on things they helped to create.

About the authors

Eva van den Broek studied Artificial Intelligence before making the leap into Natural Stupidity.* Her PhD was in experimental economics and theoretical biology and she is affiliated with Utrecht University. Eva is the founder of Behavioural Insights Netherlands and has conducted countless experiments to improve Dutch policy involving prisoners, entrepreneurs, young children, students and consumers. She regularly delivers public lectures, workshops and keynote speeches and also writes columns and blogs.

Tim den Heijer is a Dutch linguist and co-founder of B.R.A.I.N. Creatives. Tim worked for twenty years as a copywriter and creative director in the advertising industry. He worked for many of the world's best-known brands and won international prizes and nominations. He specialised in motivational campaigns, for which he increasingly took inspiration from behavioural sciences. This led to a growing conviction that big problems are only solved with a combination of science and creativity. Now he develops strategic campaigns, (brand) strategies and nudges – as a creative, but inspired by science. Tim regularly gives workshops and guest lectures.

---

* Joke poached from Amos Tversky.

Glossary: effects and technical terms

Want to know more about a particular effect? Head to the associated chapter and search for the fly!

Introduction

Butterfly effect — Little things have big consequences, like the fluttering of a butterfly's wings eventually causing a hurricane.

Effect effect — People find a phenomenon more interesting when it's termed an 'effect'.

Golden hammer effect — With your favourite tool in hand, everything suddenly looks like a nail.

Chapter 1

Delboeuf illusion — Visual illusion in which you judge the size of circles relative to their context.

Glossary: effects and technical terms

Dunning–Kruger effect People who know less about a topic overestimate themselves more than those who know more.

Forer effect The tendency to find vague, general claims about yourself convincingly descriptive, forgetting that they apply to almost everyone.

Fundamental attribution error You overestimate the chance of another person's failings being caused by character traits rather than circumstances.

Nocebo effect People taking a placebo experience the side effects of the real medicine.

Placebo effect The positive effect that a fake pill can have because you think you're taking a real medicine. Can even occur when you know you've been given a placebo.

Priming Your brain responds more strongly to something you've thought about just beforehand.

Chapter 2

Availability bias The first thing to spring to mind seems more important than it really is.

Because validation Supply a reason and people more readily agree, whether the reason is convincing or not.

Choice architecture	Nudging your choice by the way in which the options are presented: adding (or removing) extreme or nonsense options.
Complexity bias	You more readily accept a(n unnecessarily) complex explanation than a simple one.
Decoy	The ugly little brother effect: by adding an objectively less attractive option, you push people towards the other alternative.
Default	Few people make the effort to change a standard option.
Endowed progress	The more time and energy you've put into something, the harder it is to stop.
Generation effect	Information that you've generated yourself, for instance by completing a sentence, is retained better.
Illusion of explanatory depth	It feels like you get it, but try explaining how a bike's brake mechanism works.
Intention–action gap	The gap between what you intend and what you actually do.
Variable reward	An unpredictable outcome is addictive.
Zeigarnik effect	You remember unfinished tasks better than completed ones.

Glossary: effects and technical terms

Chapter 3

Ambiguity aversion — We more readily opt for a known risk than an ambiguous risk.

Anticipated regret — People try to minimise this when making decisions.

Certainty effect — People love certainty, so they shy away from small risks.

Endowment effect — Something you own seems worth more than you would be willing to spend to buy it.

Loss aversion — The pain of losing something is worse than the pleasure when you receive something of the same magnitude.

Omission bias — We more readily accept a risk that is naturally present than a 'man-made' risk.

Ostrich effect — People will sometimes make an effort and even pay to avoid certain information.

Risk avoidance — Opportunities attract less than risks repulse.

Chapter 4

Bestseller effect — The fact that a book is selling well leads to it selling more.

Competitive altruism — The tendency to compete in kind behaviour.

Moral licensing effect — After good behaviour you're more inclined to indulge in bad behaviour.

Negative social proof	The information that negative behaviour is prevalent unintentionally elicits that behaviour.
Red sneakers effect	The lack of status symbols as the ultimate status symbol: the CEO in sneakers.
Snob effect	An item becomes less attractive when many other people own one.
Social norm	What you think others in your group are doing or should be doing.
Social proof or the **bandwagon effect**	You adjust your opinion or behaviour in response to the behaviour of others.
Sucker effect	You want to see someone else doing something before you'll do it yourself (because otherwise you might end up being that one sucker who's stupid enough to do it).
Warm glow effect	Being kind feels good.
What the hell effect	After bad behaviour, you're inclined to engage in more bad behaviour.
White-coat effect or **authority**	People more readily follow instructions from someone displaying the outward signs of authority.

Glossary: effects and technical terms

Chapter 5

Commitment Committing to a resolution by attaching irreversible consequences to it.

Ego depletion The more frequently you resist temptation in a day, the more difficult it becomes to keep on doing it.

Hot/cold empathy gap People are bad at predicting how they will feel and behave in a different emotional situation.

Hyperbolic discounting See **present bias**; this overvaluation is greater when it applies between now and a week from now than between fifty-two and fifty-three weeks away.

Implementation intentions Specifying and firming up a plan in 'if-then constructions' increases the chance that you'll carry it out.

Order effect Having a preference due to the order in which options are presented, for instance the first (primacy effect) or last (recency effect).

Peak-end rule You tend to evaluate a situation in retrospect based on the emotional peak and what you felt about the end.

Present bias People overvalue rewards within their reach now compared with future rewards.

Procrastination	Putting off things you need to do.
Temptation bundling	Pairing something you like (preferably a guilty pleasure) with something you need to do and struggle to get around to, and which you wish to turn into a habit.
Vicarious goal fulfilment	Once you've found at least one option for fulfilling a good intention, you feel you have permission to make choices that go against that good intention.

Chapter 6

Focusing illusion	Something feels more important than it is as soon as you give it your attention.
Framing	The presentation of a message affects how it is evaluated.
Identifiable victim effect	A recognisable victim motivates people more than impressive figures.
Inattentional blindness	You stop noticing something that is very well known.
Keats heuristic	More attractively worded claims are more credible.
Mere-exposure effect	The more frequently you're exposed to something, the more you value it.
Narrative fallacy	The brain makes facts into stories with causes and effects.

Glossary: effects and technical terms

Pratfall	People who make (unimportant) blunders receive more respect.
Reference effect or **anchoring**	Even unrelated figures influence your valuation or estimation.
Romeo and Juliet effect	You want something because it's forbidden.
Scarcity	You want something more because it's harder to obtain.
Status symbols	Also known as **conspicuous consumption**; ostentatiously expensive goods raise status.
Veblen goods	Goods for which demand grows as the price rises.
Von Restorff effect	Anything that's different from its surroundings becomes more noticeable.

Chapter 7

Cobra effect or **law of unintended consequences**	A reward working counterproductively.
Displacement effect or **crowding out**	A reward comes at the cost of intrinsic motivation.
Goodhart's Law	An indicator of success becomes a goal in itself, it loses its usefulness as an indicator.

Conclusion

But-you-are-free effect	Emphasise freedom of choice and you increase the chance of people granting your request.

Bibliography

Introduction

1. Evans-Pritchard, B. (2013), 'Aiming to Reduce Cleaning Costs' in: *Works That Work*, no. 1, 2013.

Chapter 1

1. Poundstone, W. (2016), *Head in the Cloud: Why Knowing Things Still Matters When Facts are So Easy to Look Up.* New York: Little, Brown Spark.
2. Muller, A., L.A. Sirianni and R.J. Addante (2021), 'Neural correlates of the Dunning-Kruger effect' in: *European Journal of Neuroscience, 53* (2), 460–484.
3. Konnikova, M. (2016), *The Confidence Game: Why We Fall For It… Every time.* New York: Penguin.
4. Kurzban, R. (2012), *Why Everyone (Else) is a Hypocrite: Evolution and the Modular Mind.* Princeton, New Jersey: Princeton University Press.
5. Kross, E. (2021), *Chatter: The Voice in Our Head and How to Harness It.* New York: Random House.
6. Schwardmann, P. and J. van der Weele (2019), 'Deception and self-deception' in: *Nature Human Behaviour, 3* (10), 1055–1061.
7. Charness, G., A. Rustichini and J. van de Ven (2018), 'Self-confidence and strategic behavior' in: *Experimental Economics, 21* (1), 72–98.

8. Azucar, D., D. Marengo and M. Settanni (2018), 'Predicting the Big 5 personality traits from digital footprints on social media: A meta-analysis' in: *Personality and Individual Differences, 124*, 150–159.
9. Zarouali, B., T. Dobber, G. de Pauw and C. de Vreese (2020), 'Using a personality-profiling algorithm to investigate political microtargeting: assessing the persuasion effects of personality-tailored ads on social media' in: *Communication Research*, 0093650220961965.
10. Vedantam, S. (Host) (2018), 'Everybody lies, and that's not always a bad thing.' Hidden Brain Podcast, NPR, 9 April 2018.
11. Andreoni, J., J.M. Rao and H. Trachtman (2017), 'Avoiding the ask: A field experiment on altruism, empathy, and charitable giving' in: *Journal of Political Economy, 125* (3), 625–653.
12. Saccardo, S. and M. Serra-Garcia (2020), 'Cognitive Flexibility or Moral Commitment? Evidence of Anticipated Belief Distortion'. Working paper.
13. Kahan, Dan M., Ellen Peters, Erica Cantrell Dawson and Paul Slovic (2017). 'Motivated numeracy and enlightened self-government' in: *Behavioural Public Policy* 1, no. 1 (2017): 54–86.
14. Plassmann, H., J. O'Doherty, B. Shiv and A. Rangel (2008), 'Marketing actions can modulate neural representations of experienced pleasantness' in *Proceedings of the National Academy of Sciences, 105* (3), 1050–1054.
15. Thunström, L., J. Nordström, J.F. Shogren, M. Ehmke and K. van't Veld (2016), 'Strategic self-ignorance' in: *Journal of Risk and Uncertainty, 52* (2), 117–136.
16. Onwezen, M.C. and C.N. van der Weele (2016), 'When indifference is ambivalence: Strategic ignorance about meat consumption' in: *Food Quality and Preference, 52*, 96–105.
17. Holden, S.S., N. Zlatevska and C. Dubelaar (2016), 'Whether smaller plates reduce consumption depends on who's serving and who's looking: a meta-analysis' in: *Journal of the Association for Consumer Research, 1* (1), 134–146.
18. Karremans, J.C., W. Stroebe and J. Claus (2006), 'Beyond Vicary's

fantasies: The impact of subliminal priming and brand choice' in: *Journal of Experimental Social Psychology, 42* (6), 792–798.

Chapter 2

1. Thaler, Richard H. and Cass R. Sunstein (2008), *Nudge: Improving Decisions about Health, Wealth, and Happiness*. New Haven: Yale University Press.
2. Simon, H.A. (1971), 'Designing Organizations for an Information-Rich World' in: *Martin Greenberger, Computers, Communication, and the Public Interest*. Baltimore: The Johns Hopkins Press, p. 40–41.
3. 'Krug, S. (2005), *Don't Make Me Think: A Common Sense Approach to Web Usability*. New York: Pearson Education.
4. Deng, B. (2015), 'Papers with shorter titles get more citations' in: *Nature News*, https://www.nature.com/articles/nature.2015.18246.
5. Langer, E.J., A. Blank and B. Chanowitz (1978), 'The mindlessness of ostensibly thoughtful action: The role of "placebic" information in interpersonal interaction' in: *Journal of Personality and Social Psychology, 36* (6), 635.
6. Gigerenzer, G., R. Hertwig, E. van den Broek, B. Fasolo and K. Katsikopoulos (2005). '"A 30% chance of rain tomorrow": How does the public understand probabilistic weather forecasts?' *Risk Analysis, 25* (3), 623–629.
7. Iyengar, S.S. and M.R. Lepper (2000), 'When choice is demotivating: Can one desire too much of a good thing?' in: *Journal of Personality and Social Psychology, 79* (6), 995.
8. Chernev, A., U. Boeckenholt and J. Goodman (2015), 'Choice overload: A conceptual review and meta-analysis' in: *Journal of Consumer Psychology, 25* (2), 333–358.
9. Johnson, E.J. and D. Goldstein (2003), 'Do defaults save lives?' in: *Science, 302* (5649), 1338–1339.
10. Paunov, Y., M. Wänke and T. Vogel (2019), 'Transparency effects on policy compliance: disclosing how defaults work can enhance their effectiveness' in: *Behavioural Public Policy, 3* (2), 187–208.
11. Steeg, M. van der and I. Waterreus (2015), 'Gedragsinzichten

benutten voor beter onderwijsbeleid' (Using behavioural insights to improve education policy) in: *Economisch Statistische Berichten, 100* (4707), 219-221.
12. Eyal, N. (2014), *Hooked: How to Build Habit-Forming Products*. London: Penguin.
13. Diemand-Yauman, C., D.M. Oppenheimer and E.B. Vaughan (2011), 'Fortune favors the bold (and the italicized): effects of disfluency on educational outcomes' in: *Cognition, 118* (1), 111-115.
14. Song, H. and N. Schwarz (2008), 'If it's hard to read, it's hard to do: Processing fluency affects effort prediction and motivation' in: *Psychological Science, 19* (10), 986-988.

Chapter 3

1. Kahneman, D., J.L. Knetsch and R.H. Thaler (1990), 'Experimental Tests of the Endowment Effect and the Coase Theorem' in: *Journal of Political Economy, 98* (6), 1325-1348.
2. Knutson, B., S. Rick, G.E. Wimmer, D. Prelec and G. Loewenstein (2007), 'Neural predictors of purchases' in: *Neuron, 53* (1), 147-156.
3. Briers, B. and S. Laporte (2010), 'Empty pockets full stomachs: How monetary scarcity and monetary primes lead to caloric desire' in: *NA - Advances in Consumer Research Volume 37*, 570-571.
4. Bar-Eli, M., O. Azar and Y. Lurie (2009), '(Ir)rationality in action: do soccer players and goalkeepers fail to learn how to best perform during a penalty kick?' in: *Progress in Brain Research, Vol. 174*, 97-108.
5. Wolf, M., & Weissing, F. J. (2010). 'An explanatory framework for adaptive personality differences' in: *Philosophical Transactions of the Royal Society B: Biological Sciences, 365* (1560), 3959-3968.
6. Hintze, A., R.S. Olson, C. Adami and R. Hertwig (2015), 'Risk sensitivity as an evolutionary adaptation' in: *Scientific Reports, 5* (1), 1-7.
7. Kuhn, P.J., P. Kooreman, A.R. Soetevent and A. Kapteyn (2008), *The own and social effects of an unexpected income shock:*

evidence from the Dutch Postcode Lottery (No. w14035). National Bureau of Economic Research.

8. Odermatt, R. and A. Stutzer (2019), '(Mis-)predicted subjective well-being following life events' in: *Journal of the European Economic Association, 17* (1), 245–283.
9. Shin, J. and D. Ariely (2004), 'Keeping doors open: The effect of unavailability on incentives to keep options viable' in: *Management Science, 50* (5), 575–586.
10. Van Ittersum, K., B. Wansink, J.M. Pennings and D. Sheehan (2013), 'Smart shopping carts: How real-time feedback influences spending.' *Journal of Marketing, 77* (6), 21–36.
11. Sunstein, C.R. (2020), *Too Much Information: Understanding what You Don't Want to Know*. Cambridge, MA: MIT Press.
12. Karlsson, N., G. Loewenstein and D. Seppi (2009), 'The ostrich effect: Selective attention to information' in: *Journal of Risk and Uncertainty, 38* (2), 95–115.
13. Thunström, L. (2019), 'Welfare effects of nudges: The emotional tax of calorie menu labeling' in: *Judgment and Decision Making, 14* (1), 11.
14. Sunstein, C.R., S. Bobadilla-Suarez, S.C. Lazzaro and T. Sharot (2016), 'How people update beliefs about climate change: Good news and bad news' in: *Cornell L. Rev., 102*, 1431.

Chapter 4

1. Lessne, G.J. and E.M. Notarantonio (1988), 'The effect of limits in retail advertisements: A reactance theory perspective' in: *Psychology & Marketing, 5* (1), 33–44.
2. Salganik, M.J., P.S. Dodds and D.J. Watts (2006), 'Experimental Study of Inequality and Unpredictability in an Artificial Cultural Market' in: *Science, 311* (5762), 854–856.
3. Keizer, K., S. Lindenberg and L. Steg (2008), 'The Spreading of Disorder' in: *Science, 322* (5908), 1681–1685.
4. Liel, Y. and L. Zalmanson (2020), 'What If an AI Told You That 2+ 2 Is 5? Conformity to Algorithmic Recommendations' in:

Proceedings ICIS 2020, https://icis2020.aisconferences.org.

5. The Behavioural Insights Team (2019), 'Behavioural Insights for Building the Police Force of Tomorrow.' https://www.bi.team/wp-content/uploads/2019/01/BIT-Police-report_MKV5-WEB.pdf.
6. Bursztyn, L., A.L. González and D. Yanagizawa-Drott (2020), 'Misperceived Social Norms: Women Working Outside the Home in Saudi Arabia' in: *American Economic Review*, *110* (10), 2997–3029.
7. Sparkman, G. and G.M. Walton (2017), 'Dynamic Norms Promote Sustainable Behavior, Even If It Is Counternormative' in: *Psychological Science*, *28* (11), 1663–1674.
8. Herrmann, B., C. Thöni and S. Gächter (2008), 'Antisocial Punishment Across Societies' in: *Science*, *319* (5868), 1362–1367.
9. Thöni, C. and S. Volk (2018), 'Conditional cooperation: Review and refinement' in: *Economics Letters*, *171*, 37–40.
10. Luca, M. (2017), 'Designing online marketplaces: Trust and reputation mechanisms' in: *Innovation Policy and the Economy*, *17* (1), 77–93.
11. Edelman, B., M. Luca and D. Svirsky (2017), 'Racial Discrimination in the Sharing Economy: Evidence from a Field Experiment' in: *American Economic Journal: Applied Economics*, *9* (2), 1–22.
12. Sezer, O., F. Gino and M.I. Norton (2018), 'Humblebragging: A Distinct – and Ineffective – Self-Presentation Strategy' in: *Journal of Personality and Social Psychology*, *114* (1), 52.
13. Zahavi, A. (1990), 'Arabian Babblers: the quest for social status in a cooperative breeder' in: *Cooperative Breeding in Birds: Long Term Studies of Ecology and Behaviour*, 105–130.
14. Northover, S.B., W.C. Pedersen, A.B. Cohen and P.W. Andrews (2017), 'Artificial surveillance cues do not increase generosity: Two meta-analyses' in: *Evolution and Human Behavior*, 38 (1), 144–153.
15. Iredale, W., M. van Vugt and R. Dunbar (2008), 'Showing Off in Humans: Male Generosity as a Mating Signal' in: *Evolutionary Psychology*, *6* (3), 386–392. https://doi.org/10.1177/147470490800600302.
16. Ariely, D. (2013), *The (Honest) Truth About Dishonesty: How We*

Lie To Everyone – Especially Ourselves. London: HarperCollins.
17. Bickman, L. (1974), 'The Social Power of a Uniform' in: *Journal of Applied Social Psychology, 4* (1), 47-61.
18. Nagel, R. (1995), 'Unraveling in Guessing Games: An Experimental Study' in: *The American Economic Review, 85* (5), 1313-1326.
19. Kidd, D. and E. Castano (2019), 'Reading Literary Fiction and Theory of Mind: Three Preregistered Replications and Extensions of Kidd and Castano (2013)' in: *Social Psychological and Personality Science, 10* (4), 522-531.
20. Premack, D. and A.J. Premack (1997), 'Infants Attribute Value± to the Goal-Directed Actions of Self-propelled Objects' in: *Journal of Cognitive Neuroscience, 9* (6), 848-856.
21. Strohmetz, D.B., B. Rind, R. Fisher and M. Lynn (2002), 'Sweetening the Till: The Use of Candy to Increase Restaurant Tipping' in: *Journal of Applied Social Psychology, 32* (2), 300-309.
22. Smith, Adam (1776), *An Inquiry into the Nature and Causes of the Wealth of Nations.* London: W. Strahan.
23. Darwin, C. (1989), *The Works of Charles Darwin: The Descent of Man, and Selection in Relation to Sex* (Vol. 2). New York: NYU Press.
24. Yuan Yuan, Tracy Xiao Liu, Chenhao Tan, Qian Chen, Alex Pentland and Jie Tang (2020), 'Gift Contagion in Online Groups: Evidence from Wechat Red Packets.' Working paper, preprint www.MIT.edu.
25. Watanabe, T., M. Takezawa, Y. Nakawake, A. Kunimatsu, H. Yamasue, M. Nakamura, Y. Miyashita and N. Masuda (2014), 'Two distinct neural mechanisms underlying indirect reciprocity' in: *Proceedings of the National Academy of Sciences, 111* (11), 3990-3995.

Chapter 5

1. Mischel, W. and E.B. Ebbesen (1970), 'Attention in delay of gratification' in: *Journal of Personality and Social Psychology, 16* (2), 329.
2. Bar, M. (2010), 'Wait for the second marshmallow?

Future-oriented thinking and delayed reward discounting in the brain' in: *Neuron, 66* (1), 4–5.
3. Thunström, L., J. Nordström and J.F. Shogren (2015), 'Certainty and overconfidence in future preferences for food' in: *Journal of Economic Psychology, 51*, 101–113.
4. Chatterjee, K., S. Chng, B. Clark, A. Davis, J. De Vos, D. Ettema, S. Hardy and I. Reardon (2020), 'Commuting and wellbeing: a critical overview of the literature with implications for policy and future research' in: *Transport Reviews, 40* (1), 5–34.
5. Frey, B.S. and A. Stutzer (2018), *Economics of Happiness.* New York: Springer International Publishing.
6. Wilcox, K., B. Vallen, L. Block and G.J. Fitzsimons (2009), 'Vicarious goal fulfillment: When the mere presence of a healthy option leads to an ironically indulgent decision' in: *Journal of Consumer Research, 36* (3), 380–393.
7. Lerner, J.S. and D. Keltner (2001), 'Fear, anger, and risk' in: *Journal of Personality and Social Psychology, 81* (1), 146.
8. Buser, T. (2016), 'The impact of losing in a competition on the willingness to seek further challenges' in: *Management Science, 62* (12), 3439–3449.
9. Niederle, M. and L. Vesterlund (2007), 'Do women shy away from competition? Do men compete too much?' in: *The Quarterly Journal of Economics, 122* (3), 1067–1101.
10. Coates, J.M. and J. Herbert (2008), 'Endogenous steroids and financial risk taking on a London trading floor' in: *Proceedings of the National Academy of Sciences, 105* (16), 6167–6172.
11. Mehta, P.H. and S. Prasad (2015), 'The dual-hormone hypothesis: a brief review and future research agenda' in: *Current Opinion in Behavioral Sciences, 3*, 163–168.
12. Dai, H., K.L. Milkman, D.A. Hofmann and B.R. Staats (2015), 'The impact of time at work and time off from work on rule compliance: the case of hand hygiene in health care' in: *Journal of Applied Psychology, 100* (3), 846.
13. Linder, J.A., J.N. Doctor, M.W. Friedberg, H.R. Nieva, C. Birks, D. Meeker and C.R. Fox (2014), 'Time of day and the decision to

prescribe antibiotics' in: *JAMA Internal Medicine, 174* (12), 2029–2031.
14. Danziger, S., J. Levav and L. Avnaim-Pesso (2011), 'Extraneous factors in judicial decisions' in: *Proceedings of the National Academy of Sciences, 108* (17), 6889–6892.
15. Kahneman, D., B.L. Fredrickson, C.A. Schreiber and D.A. Redelmeier (1993), 'When more pain is preferred to less: Adding a better end' in: *Psychological Science, 4* (6), 401–405.
16. Bejan, A. (2019), 'Why the days seem shorter as we get older' in: *European Review, 27* (2), 187–194.
17. Cialdini, R. (2018), 'Why the world is turning to behavioral science' in: Samson, A., (2018), *The Behavioral Economics Guide 2018*, https://www.behavioraleconomics.com/be-guide/the-behavioral-economics-guide-2018/.
18. Goldszmidt, A., J.A. List, R.D. Metcalfe, I. Muir, V.K. Smith and J. Wang (2020), *The Value of Time in the United States: Estimates from Nationwide Natural Field Experiments* (No. w28208). National Bureau of Economic Research.
19. Mani, A., S. Mullainathan, E. Shafir and J. Zhao (2013), 'Poverty impedes cognitive function' in: *Science, 341* (6149), 976–980.
20. Shah, A.K., S. Mullainathan and E. Shafir (2012), 'Some consequences of having too little' in: *Science, 338*(6107), 682–685.
21. Autoriteit Financiële Markten (Dutch financial regulator) (AFM, 2016). 'Let op: geld lenen kost geld. Een onderzoek naar de effectiviteit van een waarschuwing in kredietreclames' (Note: borrowing money costs money. A study into the effectiveness of a warning in credit advertisements), www.afm.nl.
22. Dai, H., K.L. Milkman and J. Riis (2014), 'The fresh start effect: Temporal landmarks motivate aspirational behavior' in: *Management Science, 60* (10), 2563–2582.
23. Chen, M.K. (2013), 'The effect of language on economic behavior: Evidence from savings rates, health behaviors, and retirement assets' in: *American Economic Review, 103* (2), 690–731.
24. Reuben, E., P. Sapienza and L. Zingales (2015), 'Procrastination

and impatience' in: *Journal of Behavioral and Experimental Economics, 58*, 63–76.
25. DellaVigna, S. and U. Malmendier (2006), 'Paying not to go to the gym' in: *American Economic Review, 96* (3), 694–719.
26. Kaur, S., M. Kremer and S. Mullainathan (2015), 'Self-control at work' in: *Journal of Political Economy, 123* (6), 1227–1277.
27. Ariely, D. and K. Wertenbroch (2002), 'Procrastination, deadlines, and performance: Self-control by precommitment' in: *Psychological Science, 13* (3), 219–224.

Chapter 6

1. Strauss, N. (2005). *The Game: Penetrating the Secret Society of Pickup Artists.* New York: ReganBooks.
2. Carnegie, D. (1936). *How to Win Friends and Influence People.* New York: Simon & Schuster.
3. Goldstein, Noah, Steve J. Martin and Robert B. Cialdini (2007), *YES! 50 Secrets from the Science of Persuasion.* London: Profile Books.
4. Pennycook, G., J. Binnendyk, C. Newton and D. G. Rand (2020). 'A practical guide to doing behavioural research on fake news and misinformation.' Working paper, https://osf.io/preprints/psyarxiv/g69ha.
5. Aronson, E., B. Willerman and J. Floyd (1966), 'The effect of a pratfall on increasing interpersonal attractiveness' in: *Psychonomic Science*, 4(6), 227–228.
6. Sanford, A.J., N. Fay, A. Stewart and L. Moxey, L. (2002), 'Perspective in Statements of Quantity, with Implications for Consumer Psychology' in: *Psychological Science*, 13(2), 130–134.
7. Tversky, A. and D. Kahneman (1981), 'The Framing of Decisions and the Psychology of Choice' in: *Science, 211* (4481), 453–458.
8. Jay Heinrichs (2020), *Thank You for Arguing: What Aristotle, Lincoln, and Homer Simpson Can Teach Us About the Art of Persuasion.* United States: Crown Publishing Group.

9. McGlone, M.S. and J. Tofighbakhsh (2000), 'Birds of a Feather Flock Conjointly (?): Rhyme as reason in aphorisms' in: *Psychological Science, 11* (5), 424–428.
10. Jung, M.H., H. Perfecto and L.D. Nelson (2016), 'Anchoring in Payment: Evaluating a Judgmental Heuristic in Field Experimental Settings' in: *Journal of Marketing Research, 53* (3), 354–368.
11. Guthrie, C., J.J. Rachlinski and A.J. Wistrich (2001), 'Inside the Judicial Mind' in: *Cornell Law Review, 86* (4), 777–830.
12. Zhang, D., Y. Salant and J.A. van Mieghem (2018), 'Where Did the Time Go? On the Increase in Airline Schedule Padding Over 21 Years', working paper.
13. Glenn, Joshua and Rob Walker (2012), *Significant Others*. Seattle: Fantagraphics Books.

Chapter 7

1. Swisher III, C. C., .H. Curtis and R. Lewin (2001), *Java Man: How Two Geologists Changed Our Understanding of Human Evolution*. Chicago, IL: University of Chicago Press.
2. Dur, R. and M. van Lent (2019), 'Socially useless jobs' in: *Industrial Relations: A Journal of Economy and Society, 58* (1), 3–16.
3. Gneezy, U., J.A. List, J.A. Livingston, X. Qin, S. Sadoff and Y. Xu (2019), 'Measuring success in education: the role of effort on the test itself' in: *American Economic Review: Insights, 1* (3), 291–308.
4. Duflo, E., R. Hanna and S.P. Ryan (2012), 'Incentives work: Getting teachers to come to school' in: *American Economic Review, 102* (4), 1241–78.
5. Levitt, S.D., J.A. List, S. Neckermann and S. Sadoff (2016), 'The behavioralist goes to school: Leveraging behavioral economics to improve educational performance' in: *American Economic Journal: Economic Policy, 8* (4), 183–219.
6. Mas, A. (2016), 'Does Disclosure Affect CEO Pay Setting? Evidence from the Passage of the 1934 Securities and Exchange Act.' Working paper, Princeton University, Industrial Relations Section.

7. Ariely, D., U. Gneezy, G. Loewenstein and N. Mazar (2009), 'Large stakes and big mistakes' in: *The Review of Economic Studies, 76* (2), 451–469.
8. Cohn, A., E. Fehr and L. Goette (2015), 'Fair wages and effort provision: Combining evidence from a choice experiment and a field experiment' in: *Management Science, 61* (8), 1777–1794.
9. Falk, A., F. Kosse, I. Menrath, P.E. Verde and J. Siegrist (2018), 'Unfair pay and health' in: *Management Science, 64* (4), 1477–1488.
10. Bohnet, I. (2016), *What works*. Cambridge, MA: Harvard University Press.
11. Mellström, C. and M. Johannesson (2008), 'Crowding out in blood donation: was Titmuss right?' in: *Journal of the European Economic Association, 6* (4), 845–863.
12. Kouchaki, M., K. Smith-Crowe, A.P. Brief and C. Sousa (2013), 'Seeing green: Mere exposure to money triggers a business decision frame and unethical outcomes' in: *Organizational Behavior and Human Decision Processes, 121* (1), 53–61.
13. Falk, A. and N. Szech (2013), 'Morals and markets' in: *Science, 340* (6133), 707–711.
14. Cohn, A., E. Fehr and M.A. Maréchal (2014), 'Business culture and dishonesty in the banking industry' in: *Nature, 516* (7529), 86–89.
15. Gneezy, U. and A. Rustichini (2000), 'A fine is a price' in: *The Journal of Legal Studies, 29* (1), 1–17.
16. Halperin, B., B. Ho, J.A. List and I. Muir. (2019), *Toward an Understanding of the Economics of Apologies: Evidence from a Large-Scale Natural Field Experiment* (No. w25676). National Bureau of Economic Research.
17. Yoeli, E., M. Hoffman, D.G. Rand and M.A. Nowak (2013), 'Powering up with indirect reciprocity in a large-scale field experiment' in: *Proceedings of the National Academy of Sciences, 110* (Supplement 2), 10424–10429.
18. Brandes, L. and E. Franck (2012), 'Social preferences or personal career concerns? Field evidence on positive and negative reciprocity in the workplace' in: *Journal of Economic Psychology, 33* (5), 925–939.

Bedford Square Publishers is an independent publisher of fiction and non-fiction, founded in 2022 in the historic streets of Bedford Square London and the sea mist shrouded green of Bedford Square Brighton.

Our goal is to discover irresistible stories and voices that illuminate our world.

We are passionate about connecting our authors to readers across the globe and our independence allows us to do this in original and nimble ways.

The team at Bedford Square Publishers has years of experience and we aim to use that knowledge and creative insight, alongside evolving technology, to reach the right readers for our books. From the ones who read a lot, to the ones who don't consider themselves readers, we aim to find those who will love our books and talk about them as much as we do.

We are hunting for vital new voices from all backgrounds – with books that take the reader to new places and transform perceptions of the world we live in.

Follow us on social media for the latest Bedford Square Publishers news.

🐦 @bedsqpublishers
f facebook.com/bedfordsq.publishers/
📷 @bedfordsq.publishers

https://bedfordsquarepublishers.co.uk/